Murray Loop

Larkin,
Best wishes to you
Sincerely,

Jed W. Cox
12-21-10

Also by Ted W. Cox

*The Toledo Incident of 1925: Three Days
That Made History in Toledo, Oregon*

(Recommended by Oregon Library Association)

Available online at:
OldWorldPublications.Com.

Murray Loop
Journey of an Oregon Family
1808—1949

Ted W. Cox

Old World Publications
Corvallis, Oregon

© 2009 by Ted W. Cox

Library of Congress Cataloguing-in-Publication data
Cox, Ted W., 1947-
Murray loop—journey of an Oregon family, 1808-1949

Includes index
ISBN 978-0-9760891-3-1

1. Oregon History. 2. Lincoln County—Oregon History.
3. Newport—Oregon History. 4. Toledo—Oregon History.
5. Ohio History. 6. Missouri History. 7. Willamette Valley
History. 8. Scottish History. 9. Butter Tub. 10. Cooperage.
11. Underground Railroad. I. Title.

December 2009
Cover Art: Pastel by Minnie Owram, circa 1897

Old World Publications
Corvallis, Oregon, U.S.A.
www.oldworldpublications.com

Printed in the United States of America
United Graphics, Inc.
Chicago, Illinois

To the Memory of
Alice Phedora Murray Green
1907-1998

1. *Alice at home in Philomath, Oregon, in 1995. After almost eighty years of gardening, she is standing in the last garden she planted.*

CONTENTS

ILLUSTRATIONS

MAPS

FOREWORD

Murray Loop frames a snapshot of America growing up. Ted Cox's well-crafted tale begins with dissatisfied emigrant stirrings on the Scottish Highland heath and ends an ocean, a continent, and three generations away on the ebbing tides of the Pacific Coast. Along the way the family we come to know as the Murrays faces the facts of life: birth, marriage, divorce, death; some timely, some not.

Cox tells an intensely human tale. He also tells an honest one. In *Murray Loop*, America, too, faces its legacies. Much of the Murray story is set in Toledo—not Spain's legendary steel center or Ohio's car parts emporium—but a modest burg on the banks of Oregon's Yaquina River, best known for timber, tideland crabs, tourism, and butter barrel staves.

While great events in history—a Great War, a Great Depression, a great influenza pandemic—brush Toledo, brutal conflicts of culture confront it full-on. The spark of hope drawing European emigrants westward is stolen from the dying embers of an ancient people, driven destitute and helpless from their native lands. Cox tells that story, too.

Murray Loop is homestead country. In the rosy retrospect of Thoreau's mid-nineteenth-century idyll, homesteads grow on uncontested land, places apart, as bounties of nature. The hand-hewn cabin beside the pond, simple life in a cozy pastoral getaway, the cycle of seasons gentling daily routines to the tempos of nature—these are durable American myths. But Thoreau's contemporary Darwin comes closer to the truth.

Homesteading is a contest; strife and struggle between competing elements and interests. Some lose, some don't.

Creatures contest. Cattle and sheep, bred away from their feral ancestors, rut and ruminate in dull docility, awaiting slaughter.

The land contests. Forests and fields are cut and cleared of native species, then furrowed and set to growing crops.

Cultures contest. In Oregon, blue-coated soldiers come to clarify the worth of defaulted treaties, driving Indians to the coast and coast dwellers into the sea, then stand guard as their former lands are subdivided and deeded to squabbling land rushers. Deer path widens to hunting trail, horse track to wagon road, wagon route to rail line.

Enter the Murrays. *Murray Loop* is full of characters, likable, memorable and otherwise. At center, Minnie Alice Owram and Hugh Murray, midwestern transplants, come to Oregon in search of new lives. Minnie and Hugh are the Generation Xers of their day, born between the Civil War and the age of Robber Barons to idealist parents amid challenging times.

Forty-one-year-old Joseph Owram, vegetarian, abolitionist, visionary, former tailor of Barnsley, England, settles, unmarried, with forty-three-year-old reformed evangelist Jennie Starr on a farm outside of the "free love" community of Berlin Heights, Ohio, in the early 1860s. There, daughter Minnie Alice is born October 2, 1868. Joseph's first wife lives nearby; Jennie's ex-husband does not. All farm and champion progressive causes. With friends, Joseph plays brass in the local band, cards at home, and hides runaway slaves in the bushes. Jennie keeps house and teaches her daughter to paint and think for herself. Minnie grows and prospers; the farm and her parents' aging bodies do not.

In 1884, in search of easier times and sympathetic others, the family moves to the iconoclastic intellectual enclave of Liberal, Missouri, the Esalen of its day. The like-minded Murrays, with their sickly son Hugh, soon follow from Pictou, Nova Scotia. In Liberal, Minnie shows her mettle—by age seventeen a commercially successful photographer (and of necessity, chemist, optician, mechanic), then the farm and finance manager—when her father suddenly passes away. She cares for her frail mother, cuts her hair and hemlines short, joins Amelia Bloomer's "Rational Dress Society," and following the drought of 1895, takes the family west, to homesteading, Hugh, and more hard times. Minnie's Oregon life is simple but not easy. Neither is living with Hugh.

Hugh stays in Liberal until cupid calls and he begins romantic correspondence with Minnie in 1903. Two years later he arrives in Toledo with his violin, fertile White Wyandotte hen eggs, and a marriage proposal. All are accepted, a wedding held, and within months, Minnie's mother dies, a first child is on the way, and Hugh begins making demands. Years later, Hugh's children suggest the family tradition is one of "progressive socialism." But liberal
reform does not extend to treatment of Minnie. Hugh disapproves of her hair (too

short), her independent homesteading efforts (too long), and her friends. As years pass and the family grows, Hugh disapproves of his son's farming practices, his daughters' educational aspirations, and everyone's grammar. In contrast, Minnie tolerates much: Hugh's slovenly habits, his quick and sometimes violent temper, and his habit of sending her to sleep on the downstairs sofa when he takes in strange men with whom he sleeps upstairs. Yet through all this the Murrays get on. Hugh and Minnie may sleep apart but they work together.

Homesteading in the Murray era takes human labor, not machine management. Tools provide leverage, but arm and back and leg do the work, split the wood and prune the trees, hoe and weed and pick the crops, churn the butter, dig the outhouse, and milk the cows. Consider the cows. Twice a day, every day for years, Minnie milks five cows that produce thirty gallons—240+ pounds—of milk she then hauls, separates, stores, and later transforms into butter, cheese, and other products. Next, tend the crops, the sick. Cook, clean, haul water and hay. Mend the fence, the roof, the clothes, Minnie's near-fatal shattered hip, smashed on the horns of a berserk farm animal. At night read the children stories, and when they sleep, find solace in a few precious poems by Robert and E.B. Browning.

Years pass, children grow, marry, leave home. Hugh and Minnie labor on till age and infirmity steal their waning strength, leave the apples unpicked, the trees unpruned, the loose ends of life undone. But together they fulfill Minnie's hope, "to be of some use and do some good in the world." *Murray Loop* fulfills that hope, too.

Read this book. Listen to the fierce intelligence of a modest man telling a compelling tale of America growing up. Ted Cox runs a family restaurant in Corvallis, Oregon, the Old World Deli, a place well known for homemade chili and lasagna, progressive politics and microbrews. In another time we would recognize some of his customers. John Steinbeck would be there, offering up a yarn while Woody Guthrie gives us a tune on stage, and Dorothea Lange drops by to leave a print for the wall. These would be Ted's friends. And *Murray Loop* would be their kind of book.

Richard G. Mitchell Jr.
Corvallis, Oregon
November 2009

PREFACE

Alice Murray Green began gathering information about her family in 1937. Forty years later—around the time I met the Greens and became close to both of them—using the material collected through interviews, diaries, and letters, Alice edited and wrote a rough copy of the Murray family history.

Alice's literary zeal influenced her sister, Lucy Murray Marrs, who in 1976 also started chronicling the family history. Constance Hodges, who was gathering material for her book on Lincoln County history, *Lords of Themselves*, also motivated Lucy.

By the time Alice reached her mid-eighties, her health was beginning to fail. In 1991, eighty-four-year-old Alice wrote on the cover of one of her documents, "I am frail and forgetful, so, no more delay." Sensing that someone else would have to complete what she had started, Alice organized all of her material into cardboard boxes and neatly stored them in her bedroom. She passed away in 1998.

In 2004, her husband Roy let me see the unfinished manuscripts. After reviewing some of the material, I turned to him and said, "Have you read this stuff, Roy? It's really good." He simply replied, "Nope." Over the years Roy had watched Alice passionately researching her family history. At times he drove her to destinations to gather information, but he never became directly involved in the writing of the story. Why not? you may ask. I believe there are two reasons. First, Roy was not a bookworm like Alice. His strength lay in his ability to do things with his hands. He was a precision machinist and interested in all things mechanical. The second reason was his fear that Alice would write something negative about him. One of his comments to me was, "I hope she didn't say anything bad about me!" I assured him she hadn't.

With Roy's permission I used Alice's manuscripts, research, and family pictures as a starting point to write Murray Loop. Her words are intricately woven into the narrative. Murray Loop celebrates Alice for preserving these memories of her unforgettable family.

TWC
Corvallis, Oregon.
September 2009

ACKNOWLEDGEMENTS

During the writing of *Murray Loop* a number of people came forward to offer their encouragement and assistance. To these individuals I am deeply grateful.

First, I would like to thank Richard Mitchell Jr., Professor Emeritus of Sociology at Oregon State University, for writing the foreword. Recognized both locally and nationally for his contributions to the field of ethnography, Richard has been a consistent source of inspiration in my life for over twenty-five years. I am honored to have him open this volume.

Special thanks go to Fay Harwood and all the crew at the Old World Deli in downtown Corvallis. Individuals who have patiently witnessed my relentless passion to write this book while performing my duties as their leader.

Others to recognize include Mary Gallagher, Benton County Museum, Philomath, Oregon; Jodi Weeber and Loretta Harrison, Lincoln County Historical Society, Newport, Oregon; Robert Kentta, Cultural Resource Director of the Confederated Tribes of Siletz, Siletz, Oregon; Henry B. Zenk, Ph.D., Tribal Linguist, Confederated

Tribes of Grand Ronde; Tony A. Johnson, Cultural Education Coordinator, Confederated Tribes of Grand Ronde; Celeste Mathews, Toledo History Center, Toledo, Oregon; Lisa Miller, Nancy McFerran and the staff at the Toledo Public Library, Toledo, Oregon; Beth Camp, retired English Department faculty, Linn-Benton Community College, Albany, Oregon; Mary Finnegan, Corvallis Public Library, Corvallis, Oregon; William G. Robbins, Distinguished Professor Emeritus, History Department, Oregon State University; and Erwin Schatz, Berlin Heights Historical Society, Berlin Heights, Ohio. My thanks to all for providing information, reading drafts, and giving significant insights into local histories.

Others who helped include: Judy Juntunen, Larry Mahrt, Joan Wessell, Dixie Francis, Alan Paulsen, Linda Rehn, Ray Currier, Harland Pratt, Diane Gilliand, Bob Green, John Russell, Margaret Claracy Hartzell, Richard W. Dye, Scott Pirie, Christine M. Worman, Lynda Wigren, Pat Wilkins, Diana Allen, Terry Thayer, Jesus Alcaras, Lizanne Southgate and Adrian McBroom. All of these talented friends helped me shape *Murray Loop* into its final form.

Betty Dickason kindly gave permission to use two of her family photographs and shared some memories as a child living near the Murray farm. Old-time Murray family friends Louis Powers, Charles Burch, and Rudy Thompson were a delight to interview and willingly took the time to answer my questions.

Nancy Green Petterson, Minnie and Hugh Murray's granddaughter, has been an enthusiastic supporter of this work. She kindly provided a number of family photographs used in this volume.

Bill Murray Wilken, Minnie and Hugh's grandson, contributed not only some terrific photographs but also several insightful family stories.

Patricia Sturdevant Dye shared the lovely pastel by Minnie Murray that graces the cover of this book. I spent a delightful day with her. As we drove around Toledo, she pointed out where her relatives had lived more than one hundred years earlier.

Thanks to James P. Murray IV for technical assistance on this book.

Jane White, editor of *Murray Loop*, went over the manuscript numerous times, making corrections and suggestions. Her dedication and passion will always be appreciated.

Melissa Román, the person most important to the successful presentation of this work. Without Melissa's dedication as first reader, editor, and rewriter, the quality of the journey presented in the following pages would not have been realized. She helped to mold the story into its final form, arguing points of history, searching for details about people and incidents, writing transitions, and undertaking major editing. Melissa's skills and expert insights are imprinted throughout the book.

Last but not least, thanks go to my lifelong companion Veronica, who has waited patiently to read this volume in its completed form.

DONORS

The following friends offered financial support for the publication of *Murray Loop*:

Steven C. Lawrence

Christine M. Worman

Rodney D. Worman

Erika Lynn Worman

Jason Dean Worman

Ashley Ann Worman

Harry Demarest

Marzio Laban

Diane Laban

Barbara Kralj

Catherine Mater

Bill J. Wilken

Nancy Green Petterson

Joseph Petterson

Molly Bell

Heather Giardini

Mark Williams

Kristine Jensen

Adrian McBroom

Debbie S. Boyd

Janet O'Day

Robin Seber

Linda Rehn

Harland Pratt

1
The Patriarch—
"See your future wife."

The Murray family name had been established in The Highlands of northeast Scotland for more than 600 years when this story begins in 1808.[1] The seminal event— the introduction of the fully grown Hugh Murray to his newly born cousin Jane—is recounted in a letter written in 1953 by their granddaughter Dr. Mary MacKenzie Smith:

> Grandfather was 18 years older than Grandmother. When Grandmother was born in 1808, the midwife brought the baby out to show Grandfather, saying, "See your future wife." The young man scoffed at the idea.[2]

The midwife's prediction proved accurate. Although the teenage Hugh derided the statement made by the midwife, his descendants would pay more attention to this type of insight. Mary Smith's letter continues:

> We believe [Hugh and Jane] were cousins. On January 12, 1827, they were married. This was in the Parish of Resolis, near Cromarty, Scotland. In the Highlands of Ross-shire.[3]

Their marriage in 1827 started the patriarchal family line at the heart of *Murray Loop.*

The couple lived in the northeast Highland region owned by agrarian reformer Granville Leveson-Gower. Leveson-Gower became the Duke of Sutherland and one of the richest men in Great Britain. He held great power over the Murrays.[4]

With the last traces of Europe's feudal system ending, the early 1800s were disastrous times for many tenant farmers throughout northern Scotland. Commonly shared property, which included individual farms and small communities, were privatized into larger holdings owned by gentry. With this reorganization of land, the aristocracy no longer recognized traditional feudal responsibilities to their dependent tenants. The Murrays were caught in the conflict. Like so many of their Highland neighbors, they had little say over the changes forced on them.

A. *Scotland*

Many reformation landowners evicted peasant farmers, whose rents brought in little revenue. These families were removed

3

to make room for sheep herding, a much more profitable venture at that time. Portions of the cleared lands were later redesignated as hunting grounds for British aristocrats.

The disenfranchised Highlanders lacked legal protection under Scottish law and often received little mercy from the empowered landowners. Although some of the aristocracy provided economic incentives to induce families to leave their homes, there were other, less accommodating gentry who used violence to clear their lands. Anyone who refused to leave these farms, whether because of stubbornness or a lack of any place to go, faced brutal consequences. Historical records tell of people dying from exposure, freezing to death after the destruction of their homes during winter evictions.[5] Many displaced Highlanders sought jobs in urban factories. Others resettled on the Scottish coast to work in fisheries. Still other individuals and families emigrated overseas.[6]

The *Clearances*, a term used for these infamous expulsions, took place between 1780 and 1850, a period coinciding with the early years of the Industrial Revolution. The mass removal left thousands of men, women, and children impoverished.[7] Uprooted during one of the later evictions, Hugh and Jane Murray were financially desperate in 1840. With few opportunities available in the Highland, they looked for a new place to make their home. One of their most likely prospects meant leaving Scotland altogether.

During the previous several decades, Canadian land grants had given many disadvantaged Highlanders the opportunity to settle in the New World. Several of the Murray clan had been among those early immigrants. In 1840, Hugh wrote to his brother in Canada requesting the travel money needed for the Murrays to emigrate. His brother agreed to the loan.

In 1841, fifty-two-year-old Hugh, thirty-three-year-old Jane, thirteen-year-old Ann, ten-year-old Isabella, nine-year-old Jane, five-year-old Margaret, and three-year-old David left Cromarty, Scotland, to build a future on the other side of the Atlantic. They traveled with a large group of Highlanders aboard the 323-ton cargo ship *Lady Gray*.[8] The journey held more challenges than the Murrays expected.

Due to stormy weather, the *Lady Gray* was delayed at sea. Food became scarce and a number of passengers came down with typhus.[9] The frightening outbreak afflicted vulnerable passengers crammed together in a cargo ship not intended for passenger transport. As the captain and crew struggled to reach the Canadian shore, everyone was anxious to leave the ship.

The *Lady Gray* arrived at Pictou, Nova Scotia, on July 16, 1841.[10] The distressed passengers found a small, rugged township ill-prepared to deal with sickness. Without a local hospital to tend to the sick, the passengers called on the port doctor for help. All those aboard were removed to shore and quarantined. To keep the disease from spreading, the crew sanitized the ship while the passengers cleansed themselves. After two months, twenty-six people were ill and six were dead, among them the port doctor who had caught typhus while tending his patients.

As a young mother with five children, Jane Murray struggled to keep her family healthy in the primitive environment of Pictou. Relatives living nearby provided whatever help they could. The Murrays were lucky. None of them became ill.

By fall the ship was ready to continue the journey to Quebec. Of the approximately 245 passengers aboard the *Lady Gray,* only seventy-five originally booked passages to Pictou. The remaining passengers, including the Murrays, had planned to land at Quebec.

Once cleared from quarantine, however, most of the continuing families refused to board ship. They hesitated in part because their shipboard journey had been so disastrous, but also because many had grown to like the area around Pictou.

Murray cousins encouraged Hugh and Jane to settle nearby. The couple agreed to stay. Before parting from their shipboard companions, Hugh, along with several other heads of households, signed a formal complaint against the ship's owners protesting the group's experience aboard the *Lady Gray*.[11]

With no money and few amenities at hand, Hugh and Jane established a homestead in the nearby Toney River District on Protection Road on the Big Caribou River. They endured many hardships as they improved their land in hopes that their homestead would one day support the family:

> Trees & brush were cleared [and] an orchard & garden planted when clearing was done. A sparkling creek ran close by for good water. Gradually the family managed. Men could find work in coal mines or fishing. Both dangerous [jobs] & poor income . . .

Grandfather Hugh preached at different places, as at that time there were no nearby churches.[12]

While Hugh earned additional income working away from the farm, Ann and Isabella brought in a bit of sorely needed cash working closer to home:

> The family put in some very hard years before they had the land cleared for farming. The older girls worked in homes, cooking & [doing] housework to earn a small wage to help them buy provisions until the farm was established.[13]

By working together, the family gradually made the homestead a success.

After twenty years in Pictou, Hugh died in 1862 at the age of seventy-three. Jane was fifty-four.

In 1865, twenty-seven-year-old son David married thirty-year-old Lydia Ann Sellers. The newlyweds settled on a farm eight miles outside of Pictou. David and Lydia raised five children. Their first daughter, Sarah, was born in 1866. Hugh, their first son and the future patriarch of *Murray Loop*, was born on June 18, 1867. Sister Adaline, brother Simon, and baby sister Emma followed. The siblings grew up enjoying a close bond that they shared throughout their lives.

1
Notes

1. "Clan History," Murray Clan Society, http://www.clanmurray.org (accessed May 16, 2008). The Murray clan traces its heritage back to the twelfth century and takes its name from the province of Moray, once a local kingdom in northern Scotland. At that time, Moray included parts of what later became Inverness-shire, Nairn, and Ross-shire. One leading line of the Murrays took the surname of Sutherland, and by 1235 its descendants were called the Earls of Sutherland.
2. Dr. Mary MacKenzie Smith to Alice Murray Green, 27 September 1953.
3. Ibid.
4. After Sutherland's death in 1833, that power was passed to his son George.
5. *Wikipedia, the Free Encyclopedia,* s.v. "HighlandClearances,"http://en.wikipedia.org/wiki/highlandclearances (accessed September 12, 2006).
6. The immigration to North America was quite significant. Today there are more descendants of northern Scotland living in Canada than in Scotland.
7. *Wikipedia, the Free Encyclopedia,* s.v. "Highland Clearances" (accessed May 16, 2008).

8. George MacLaren, *The Pictou Book: Stories of Our Past* (New Glasgow, Nova Scotia: Hector Publishing, 1954), 104-105.

9. Also known as ship fever, typhus occurred in unsanitary, overcrowded conditions aboard ships. Typhus results from bacteria spread to humans through lice or fleas.

10. "Brig *Lady Gray*," Immigrant Ships Transcribers Guild, http://www.immigrantships.net/1800/ladygray410716.html (accessed May 13, 2008).

11. Research did not reveal the exact details of this formal complaint.

12. Alice Murray Green, "Memoirs" (unpublished manuscript in the author's possession, 1977).

13. Dr. Mary MacKenzie Smith to Alice Murray Green, 27 September 1953.

2
The Oregon Country

In 1841, when Hugh Murray and his family were emigrating from Scotland to eastern Canada, large numbers of people from the United States were beginning to migrate across the Great Plains to settle in the Pacific Northwest.[1] Their destination was the fertile land of the Willamette Valley in the southwest section of the Oregon Country. The Oregon Country, through treaty, was claimed at that time by both the United States and Great Britain.[2] The Willamette Valley runs north and south between the peaks of the Cascade Mountain Range and the hills of the Coast Range fifty plus miles to the west. Articles and advertisements placed in eastern newspapers and magazines during the 1830s and 40s enticed immigration by describing the fertile valley as a Garden of Eden containing rich arable farmland, temperate climate, ample water, and beautiful rainbows. With over

200 frost-free days each year, the valley was a vision of paradise.

B. *The Oregon Country, 1846. Dashed lines indicate 1859 boundaries for the state of Oregon.*

In 1841, there were about 150 U.S. citizens living in the Oregon Country.[3] Between 1841 and 1848, over 12,000 people made the five- to six-month journey west.[4] As these people arrived they disbanded and began to lay claim to the land. When wagon trains first arrived, settlers claimed land

14

located in the northern section of the valley. During the following years, settlers spread south, eventually occupying the entire 120-mile length of the Willamette. Homesteads were established; cabins erected; crops planted. The newcomers were determined to create successful farms and towns.

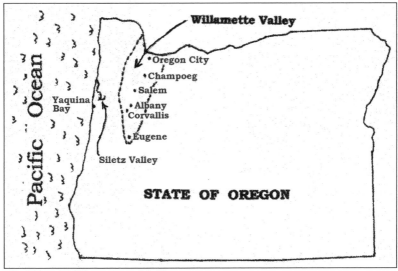

C. The Willamette Valley

Upon their arrival in the valley, settlers met scattered bands of Native Americans still reeling from the effects of devastating diseases.[5] In the most recent Willamette Valley epidemic, malaria[6] had reduced the Indian population from about 15,000 in 1830 to 600 by 1840.[7] Although Native Americans, whose ancestors had lived in the

Pacific Northwest for thousands of years, viewed the arrival of the settlers with dread,[8] they were not numerous enough to offer physical resistance.[9] At the same time many settlers viewed the native tragedy as an indication that it was the destiny of the United States to settle the Oregon Country. U.S. settlers were confident that their government would eventually support them as they seized Native land without regard to the rights of the Indians.[10]

Elijah White led the first wagon train with more than 100 people into the Willamette Valley in 1842. Native leaders were directed to him for an explanation. Acting as the first appointed Indian agent in the Pacific Northwest, White assured Willamette Valley tribal leaders that a U.S. representative bearing gifts would eventually arrive to compensate them for the loss of their homelands.[11] Local bands accepted his promise in good faith but were guarded about the changes taking place. They watched their land become lined with fences, saw their food resources dwindle, and witnessed the arrival of yet more settlers each year.[12]

While the number of homesteads grew and reshaped life in the valley, the initial cooperation and friendship between the newcomers and Native people gave way to tension and agitation. Outnumbered by the settlers, the Native Americans could do little to stop the changes taking place other than speak out in protest.

In 1843, settlers from both the United States and Great Britain held a meeting at Champoeg in the northern Willamette Valley.[13] They met to discuss the formation of an interim government to regulate and guard the interests of the recently arrived U.S. immigrants, especially their large land claims.[14] Several meetings had taken place at Champoeg since 1841 to discuss various problems and concerns. This particular meeting culminated in the establishment of a provisional legislative body with the authority to establish land claim laws, levy taxes, build roads, authorize ferries, pass laws, and even declare war.[15]

Before the Champoeg Conference, the governing legal system in the Oregon Country varied by nationality. Native tribes had customs that managed their needs, while British subjects were under jurisdiction of the Hudson Bay Company. On more uncertain ground were the U.S. settlers who were under no jurisdiction, except perhaps the Hudson Bay Company. Living outside their national boundary, they were building homes on disputed soil. Technically with no rights of their own, they were in effect squatters, people living on land they didn't own. The Champoeg Conference established the Provisional Government, which among other things formalized U.S. settler claims and Canadian claims of up to 640 acres of land for married couples.[16]

The Provisional Government had no legal constitutional relationship to the British or American government; nevertheless, British and American interests were beginning to alienate indigenous people from their land.[17]

In 1846, representatives from the United States and Britain negotiated a boundary treaty at the 49th parallel. Claim to the area known as the Oregon Country was divided between the two countries. The northern half became the British-controlled Columbia District; the southern portion remained the Oregon Country and was under U.S. control. Two years later, the U.S. Congress passed the Oregon Territorial Act, which among other stipulations provided civil institutions to protect American citizens. The territorial act theoretically protected Native American rights as well.[18]

In 1849, Joseph Lane was appointed the first territorial governor of the Oregon

Territory. When Governor Lane arrived in the Willamette Valley in March 1849, local Indians went to him expecting presents and payments for their occupied lands as promised by Elijah White seven years earlier. The Indians were flabbergasted and distraught to discover that no provision had been made for their compensation.[19] The encounter alerted Lane to a critical problem. Homesteading, according to United States law, was legal only on land that lay in the public domain. Since the U.S. had not yet negotiated to end Native land rights, the Willamette Valley did not yet qualify for legal settlement. In 1849, the Willamette Valley was still technically Indian country. Recognizing the importance of transferring the Willamette Valley from Native land rights to the public domain, Lane sent a report to Washington, D.C., urging Congress to act quickly.

Lane wasn't the only one concerned about real estate. Thousands of settlers wanted to ensure federal recognition of their existing claims under U.S. law.

Samuel Thurston, elected in 1849 as the first Oregon Territorial delegate to the U.S. Congress, went to Washington to lobby to secure an immediate and decisive resolution to the land claims.[20] Through his efforts,

Congress passed the Oregon Donation Land Act in September 1850. The act had two immediate benefits for people interested in establishing themselves in the Oregon Territory: 1) the legislation recognized prior claims made by early settlers, and 2) the act promised free land to any newly arriving settlers through November 1855.[21] By the time the act expired, close to 30,000 immigrants had entered the territory.[22]

The problem for the Indian community lay in the conflict between the Territorial Act of 1848, which acknowledged Indian possession of land, and the 1850 Donation Land Act, which opened the land to settlement.[23] The Donation Land Act contained two disastrous consequences for the Indian communities: First, the popular legislation ignored Indian land entitlement;[24] and second, the legislation offered even more Indian land for settlement by U.S. citizens. This act only exacerbated the conflicts between tribal groups and homesteaders. Congress had more work to do.

In 1850, Congress appointed Anson Dart as the superintendent of Indian affairs for the Oregon Territory, relieving Governor Joseph Lane of de facto responsibility.[25] Dart had control of the agency budget and responsibility to organize, monitor, and manage relations with all Native groups in the territory. Concurrent with Dart's appointment, a special three-man Indian commission was established to negotiate land entitlements with Willamette Valley tribes and oversee Native relocation onto reservations.[26] Negotiations were scheduled to begin in February 1851. Although the commissioners entered negotiations with the expectation of congressional support, in an unforeseen turn of events Congress abolished the commission two months before the scheduled meetings began. Unaware of their change in status, the commissioners moved forward as directed. Thus the era of treaty making in the Oregon Territory began under dubious circumstances.

As a result of the negotiations, six treaties were signed and six temporary reservations were established on the margins of the Willamette Valley. Tribal groups were restricted to these reservations. The treaties were never recognized. Native American leaders had acted in good faith only to learn later that their trust had been betrayed. Furthermore, due to restriction of movement and dwindling food resources, the valley Indians were finding survival ever more difficult. Their situation was moving from bad to worse.

On July 19, 1851, Dart wrote a letter to Indian Commissioner Luke Lea in Washington, D.C., asking for his advice in dealing with the situation:

> In reference to the awkward position in which our government is placed in Oregon, I allude to what is called the Oregon Land Bill, in which Government is bound to give to every actual settler in Oregon three hundred and twenty acres of land or six hundred and forty to a man and his wife at the same time every acre of this land is owned and occupied by a people that the Government has always acknowledged to be the bona fide and rightful owner of the soil. These facts, however, are not known to the Indians, nor do they know the fact that the Government has never forced the Indians from their lands without first having bought them. Were these two facts well understood by the Indians of this country, the end of the trouble growing out of it could not be foreseen.[27]

The Willamette Valley treaties marked the beginning of three counterproductive years for Superintendent Dart.

With the dissolution of the Indian commission, Dart himself had the sole authority to negotiate treaties. He continued to negotiate in other parts of the territory. All of his work met with similar rejection by Congress. Dart resigned in June 1853, frustrated by the lack of support from Congress that had kept him from establishing a workable Indian policy during his tenure. From the Native American perspective, the U.S. Indian policy was a sham!

Congress next appointed Joel Palmer as superintendent of Indian affairs. Palmer continued the federal policy of race separation, convinced that relocation was the only way to save Native people from extinction. He set about creating new treaties along with newly appointed Isaac Stevens, governor of the recently established Washington Territory.

During the winter of 1854-55, Indians of the Umpqua Valley and the Willamette Valley were asked once again to negotiate entitlement of their lands. Again, on November 29, 1854, and January 4, 1855, they consented.[28] A diverse group of Native Americans was sent to what was supposed to be a temporary settlement at a small valley in the Coast Range known as Grand

Ronde. Grand Ronde was one part of the huge new Coast Indian Reservation. The assemblage included over fourteen tribes that spoke at least eight different languages: Northern Kalapuya, Central Kalapuya, Southern Kalapuya, Clackamas Upper Chinook, Molalla, Upper Umpqua Athabaskan, Takelma, and Shasta.[29]

With the extinguishment of Indian land title in the Willamette Valley that land now lay in the public domain. With devastating consequences for the Indians, a resolution of the technically precarious land title question had finally taken place.

2
Notes

1. Mike Trinklein, *Jumping Off on the Oregon Trail,*http://www.isu.edu/~trinmich/indepen dence.html (accessed June 15, 2009). During the early 1840s many emigrants set out from Independence, Missouri, crossing through what are now the states of Kansas, Nebraska, Wyoming, Idaho, and into Oregon. Other points of departure came into use during the ensuing years.
2. Dorothy O. Johansen, *Empire of the Columbia* (New York: Harper & Row, 1967), 108-121. The Oregon Country in 1840 lay between the Russian-dominated north and the Spanish-dominated south, encompassing present-day British Columbia, Oregon, Washington, Idaho, and parts of Montana and Wyoming. The United States, Great Britain, Spain, Russia, and France originally claimed the Oregon Country. France lost its claim to the area after 1763. Spain gave up its claim in 1790 and 1819. Russia gave up its claim in 1824 and 1825. The United States and Great Britain agreed to joint control of the Oregon Country in 1818 and again in 1827 until 1846 when the two countries agreed to set a national boundary line at the 49th parallel. The boundary has remained to this day.

3. William G. Robbins, *Oregon: This Storied Land* (Portland: Oregon Historical Society Press, 2005), 43.
4. William E. Hill, *The Oregon Trail, Yesterday and Today* (Caldwell, ID: The Caxton Printer, Ltd., 1987), xxv.
5. Michael R. Haines and Richard H. Steckel, eds., *A Population History of North America* (Cambridge, UK: Cambridge University Press, 2000), 736. Old World diseases introduced to Native American populations by trappers, missionaries and settlers included: bubonic plague, cholera, malaria, measles, pneumonia, scarlet fever, smallpox, typhoid, whooping cough, yellow fever, and various venereal diseases.
6. William G. Robbins, *Landscapes of Promise: The Oregon Story, 1800-1940* (Seattle: University of Washington Press, 1997), 58-60.
7. Robert Boyd, *The Coming of the Spirit of Pestilence – Introduced Infectious Diseases and Population Decline among Northwest Coast Indians 1774-1874* (Seattle: University of Washington Press, 1999), 244. For over ten thousand years a variety of Native American ethnic groups migrated to and through the Pacific Northwest. After centuries of occupation, their legacy had brought a huge diversity of languages and cultures to the area. Although exact figures are unclear, historians estimate that in 1780 there were over 60,000 Native Americans living within today's Oregon state boundaries. By 1800 that number had decreased to 45,000.

8. Harold Mackey, *The Kalapuyans* (Salem, OR: Mission Mill Museum Association, 2004), 89.

9. William G. Robbins, "The Indian Question in Western Oregon: The Making of a Colonial People," in *Experiences in a Promised Land: Essays in Pacific Northwest History,* ed. G. Thomas Edwards and Carlos A. Schwantes (Seattle: University of Washington Press, 1986) 56.

10. Ibid., 64.

11. Johansen, 186. Elijah White came to Oregon thinking he was a presidentially appointed Indian agent for the territory. (Unknown to him at the time, his appointment had been cancelled when he was en route to the Northwest.) Meanwhile, he went about his business as though he were the official Indian agent for the Oregon Country. White's promises to the Indians of the Northwest were premature since neither the United States nor Great Britain held sovereignty over the Oregon Country in 1842.

12. C.F. Coan, "The First Stage of the Federal Indian Policy in the Pacific Northwest, 1849-1852," *Oregon Historical Society* (March 1922): 50.

13. Champoeg is located between Portland and Salem at the present site of Champoeg State Park.

14. The Provisional Government operated as a limited functioning body.

15. Johansen, 188-189.

16. *Encyclopaedia Britannica Online,* s.v. "Johnson v. M'Intosh, 21 U.S. 543 (1823)," http://www.britannica.com/EBchecked/topi

c/1397857/Johnson-v-MIntosh (accessed May 20, 2009). As a guide the Provisional Government used United States law, which held that Native Americans could sell their lands to the government only, not to private citizens.

17. Robbins, *Oregon: This Storied Land*, 47.
18. Ibid.
19. Mackey, 89.
20. Robbins, *Oregon: This Storied Land*, 49.
21. Robbins, *Landscapes of Promise*, 83.
22. Robbins, "The Indian Question in Western Oregon," 55.
23. Terrence O'Donnell, *An Arrow in the Earth* (Portland: Oregon Historical Society Press, 1991), 175.
24. Robbins, "The Indian Question in Western Oregon," 54.
25. Mackey, 96.
26. Mackey, 98, 151.
27. Letters received by the Office of Indian Affairs, 1824-1880. National Archives. Microcopy 234, Roll 607 NADP Document DI0.
28. Mackey, 151.
29. Confederated Tribes of Grand Ronde Cultural Resources Staff Afterword to Mackey, 188. Grand Ronde was made a permanent reservation on June 30, 1857.

3
Coast Indian Reservation

Following the federal government's resolution of Willamette Valley land title, Joel Palmer focused on confederating the Indians of the Willamette Valley, Umpqua, and Oregon coast on a reservation removed from the growing inland communities.

The Oregon coast is separated from the Willamette Valley by the Coast Range Mountains. In 1855, the central Oregon coast was still Indian country (not in the public domain). Due to perceived isolation, rough terrain, and limited agricultural potential, incoming settlers had avoided going to the area.

Hoping to prevent settler encroachment of the central Oregon coast, Palmer placed the following public notice in the *Oregon Statesman* on April 28, 1855:

Indian Reservation

Notice is hereby given, that I have designated as an Indian Reservation for the Coast and Willamette Tribes, and such others as may hereafter be located thereon, the following-described district of country:

Beginning on the shore of the Pacific Ocean, at the mouth of a small stream [Siltcoos River] about midway between the Umpqua and Siuslaw Rivers; thence easterly to the ridge dividing the waters of these streams, and along said ridge on high land to the western boundary of the eighth range of townships west of the Willamette meridian; thence north to said boundary to a point due east of Cape Lookout; thence west to the Ocean; and thence along the coast to the place of beginning.

The Tract described presents few attractions to the white settler, while it is believed to be better adapted for the colonization of the Indians than any other portion of Territory west of the Cascade Mountains affording so few facilities of settlement to our citizens.

The object of this notice is to inform the public that this reservation will not be subject to settlement by whites.

Dayton, O.T., April 17, 1855[1]

The proposed reservation was in line with policies established by Congress, and, to Palmer's way of thinking, would protect native rights from being trampled by settler expansion. In retrospect, Palmer's conviction was naïve.

On November 9, 1855, President Franklin Pierce issued an executive order officially creating the Coast Indian Reservation.[2] The upper half of the reservation stretched north to Cape Lookout and included the traditional homelands of the Tillamook, Nestucca, and Yaquina Indians. The lower half of the reservation extended south from the Yaquina tributary to include the traditional homelands of the Alsea, Coos, Siuslaw, and Lower Umpqua Indians. In all, the area encompassed nearly 1.4 million acres.[3]

Similar to Joel Palmer's posting in the *Oregon Statesman* six months earlier, the president's order centered the reservation around Yaquina Bay, but it encompassed an area approximately sixty miles north and sixty miles south along the Oregon coast. The Pacific Ocean formed the reserve's western boundary, while the eastern edge lay twenty miles inland.[4]

Three forts were constructed near the border of the reservation. Fort Yamhill, east of Grand Ronde; Fort Hoskins, east of Siletz; and Fort Umpqua, near the southern boundary.[5]

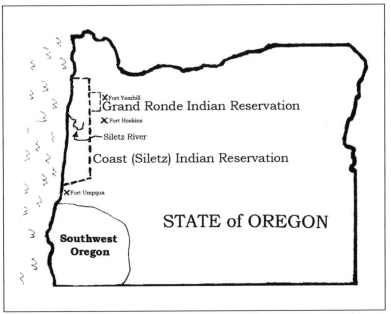

D. Coast and Grand Ronde Indian Reservations, 1854-1857. Dashed lines show their approximate boundaries.

Located within the heart of the reservation, just ten miles northeast of Yaquina Bay, lay the Siletz Valley. The valley's original population had been reduced by disease to just a handful of families by 1855. Five thousand acres of meadowland rich in soil with fresh water and open prairies were available for the relocation.[6]

Plans for resettlement altered when war broke out in southwest Oregon in October 1855. Referred to as the Rogue River Indian War, the fight was a continuation of troubles dating from 1851 with the discovery of gold in the area. The resulting flood of miners and settlers had disrupted the Native American way of life, and conflict followed.

For seven months during the winter of 1855-56, the Rogue River War dragged on in a series of violent encounters between Native American bands and the regular army working with the Oregon Volunteers. Non-combatants on both sides were killed. Hostilities occurred in the Rogue River Valley, Umpqua Valley, and along the southern Oregon coast.

The Rogue River War caused Palmer to reconsider his plans of moving Willamette Valley tribes to the coast. His new priority was protecting peaceful Indians in southwest Oregon who were in harm's way by relocating them to Grand Ronde some 200 miles to the north. He also planned to move all the warring Indians north following hostilities. Further, Palmer decided that the Grand Ronde Valley would become the permanent home for the Indians of the Willamette Valley.[7]

When the conflict ended in May 1856, 2,000 Native American men, women, and children were escorted north. Tribal groups included Takelma, Coquille, Upper Umpqua, Shasta, Chetco, Tututni, and Galice Creek

Indians.[8] At least twenty different languages and dialects were spoken by these people.[9] The first group of war survivors was taken to Dayton in June 1856. From there they walked thirty miles southwest to Grand Ronde on the edge of the Willamette Valley. Next, they were moved to the Oregon coast at the Salmon River,[10] just north of today's Lincoln City, where they stayed about a month before moving south to Yaquina Bay and the Siletz Valley.[11]

Before the resettlement could be completed Joel Palmer was relieved of his duties as superintendent of Indian affairs. Absalom F. Hedges was appointed as his replacement. Hedges continued Palmer's policy.

A small number of Yaquina Indians were living quietly at the mouth of Yaquina Bay[12] when in August 1856 relocated groups started arriving. Eleven hundred people set up temporary camps along the lower Yaquina Bay.[13] Other incoming Indians were sent straight to the Siletz Valley ten miles further northeast.[14]

In the government's haste to remove these people from their homelands, little to no preparation to receive them had been made.[15] Worse, since they were sent north with virtually no property of their own, they were dependent upon the government to supply what they could not provide for themselves. Tribal groups had to make their own shelters and gather much of their own food. During the summer months the people kept warm at night, but they faced constant food shortages.

Lt. Phil Sheridan was in the Yaquina Bay area to monitor Indian movement at that time. In his memoirs he describes the challenges faced by many of the people:

> In the summer of 1856, and while I was still on duty there, the . . . Indians on the Siletz, and down near the Yaquina Bay, became on account of hunger and prospective starvation, very excited and exasperated. . . At times their only food was rock oysters, clams and crabs. Great quantities of these shell-fish could be gathered in the bay near at hand, but the mountain Indians did not take kindly to mollusks, and indeed, ate the shell fish only as a last resort.[16]

Sheridan goes on to depict women and children harvesting crab:

> Crab catching at night on the Yaquina Bay by the Coast Indians was a picturesque scene. It was mostly done by the squaws and children, each equipped with a torch in one hand and

a sharp pointed stick in the other to take and lift the fish into baskets slung on the back to receive them. I have seen at times hundreds of squaws and children wading about in Yaquina Bay taking crabs in this manner and the reflection by the water of the light from the many torches, with the movements of the Indians while at work, formed a weird and diverting picture of which we were never tired.[17]

Sheridan may not have tired from viewing the crab harvest, but the waters of the Yaquina are not warm and the winds are not always gentle. Catching crab at night would have been a cold and uncomfortable activity, especially with the onset of winter.

Fall rains began the first week of October that year, shutting down trails from the valley and thus potential food supply routes from the interior.[18] Adding to everyone's frustration, a badly needed shipment of flour was lost in a shipwreck at the mouth of Siletz Bay in mid-December.[19]

2. Second Lieutenant Philip H. Sheridan (1831-1888), ca. 1853.

Superintendent Hedges asked Congress to release funds to support the reservation, but the political pocketbook was closed. With an insufficient budget Hedges hired Palmer to construct buildings and plant crops at the Siletz Agency. During the winter of 1856, a blacksmith shop and a water-powered sawmill were built to aid in the construction of agency buildings.

After enduring a difficult first winter, tribal leaders held council. Many decided to return to their homelands when spring approached.[20] Fleeing down the coast was the only practical option available to the desperate Indians.

Discovering the plan, the army decided to station a group of soldiers at the mouth of Yaquina Bay. Setting up a post at the harbor would give the soldiers the opportunity to act quickly if anyone tried to leave the reservation. So the army constructed a temporary blockhouse. In charge of this project was Lt. Sheridan. He chose to build on a bench of land on the north side of the bay. Today, the United States Coast Guard Station in Newport is located on this spot. The flat open area was sheltered from the unforgiving northwest winter weather by a bluff of sandstone 130 feet high and commanded a southerly view at the mouth of the bay.

Before construction could begin, Sheridan had to negotiate use of the land. The Yaquina Indians buried their dead in this place:

> It was the mortuary ground [containing about fifty above ground canoes] of these Indians that occupied the only level spot we could get. . . I made known to the Indians that we would have to take this piece of ground for the blockhouse. . .[21]

After some discussion, the Native elders had no choice but to agree to relocate the remains:

> . . .when the tide was going out, I should take my men and place the canoes in the bay and let them float out on the tide across the ocean to the happy hunting-grounds.[22]

With burial remains removed, construction of the blockhouse began immediately.

Winter gave way to spring and the pre-planned escape attempts began. Escaping Indians traveled in small groups but were quickly caught by soldiers and returned to Yaquina Bay. As the weather improved and trails inland became passable, most of the Indians living along the bay were moved to the Siletz Agency.

Getting supplies onto the reservation took organization. Overland routes from the valley were expensive and impossible once the rains started. Everything had to be transported via the waterways. Although an original supply route accessed the Siletz River by sea twenty-five miles north of the Yaquina harbor, entering Siletz Bay proved to be too dangerous. The Yaquina River offered the most reliable and economic route for delivering goods.

Supply schooners arriving at Yaquina Bay traveled thirteen miles up the river to the mouth of a large stream that quickly became known as Depot Slough. Supplies were taken two miles up the slough and offloaded at a supply depot.[23] The cargo was then hauled along a trail to the Siletz Agency eight miles further. At first the trail leading to Siletz wasn't wide enough for a wagon, so Native women were employed to pack supplies Within three years the trail was enlarged to accommodate wagons.

In all, the number of Native Americans originally brought to the Coast Indian Reservation was about 2,600. Because the early years there were so difficult, the number of individuals living on the reservation dwindled. By 1885, the population of the Coast Indian Reservation, renamed the Siletz Reservation, numbered only 900. Some individuals had moved off the reservation, but most had died from disease and poor health care.[24]

The federal policy of racial separation may have satisfied the settlers in 1856, but without political power, Native Americans, like the tenant Highlanders of Scotland, paid a brutally high price.

3
Notes

1. Joel Palmer, "Indian Reservation," *Oregon Statesman,* April 28, 1855.
2. Robert Kentta, "Our History," Confederated Tribes of Siletz Indians of Oregon, http://www.ctsi.nsn.us (accessed June 9, 2007).
3. E.A. Schwartz, *The Rogue River Indian War and Its Aftermath, 1850-1980* (Norman: University of Oklahoma Press, 1997), 162. In 1865, the Yaquina Tract was opened to non-Native settlement by presidential order. This reduced the reservation in size by about 200,000 acres. The Yaquina Track also physically divided the reservation into a southern, or Alsea, portion and a northern, or Siletz, portion. In 1875 the northern end of the Siletz portion of the reservation and the entire Alsea portion of the reservation were opened to non-Native settlement, reducing the reservation size by over one million acres. What remained became known as the Siletz Reservation. In 1892 the Siletz Reservation was further reduced by over 191,000 acres through a government mandate known as the Allotment Act.
4. Kentta, "Our History."
5. Royal A. Bensell, *All Quiet on the Yamhill: The Civil War in Oregon* (Eugene: University of Oregon Books, 1959), 206-7, 213.

6. Lionel Youst and William R. Seaburg, *Coquelle Thompson, Athabaskan Witness: A Cultural Biography* (Norman: University of Oklahoma Press, 2002), 54, 56.
7. Terrence O'Donnell, *An Arrow in the Earth* (Portland: Oregon Society Historical Press, 1991), 234. A presidential executive order officially established the Grand Ronde Reservation on June 30, 1857.
8. Oscar Hoop, "A History of Fort Hoskins" (master's thesis, University of Oregon, 1928), 69.
9. Youst and Seaburg, 133.
10. Schwartz, 164.
11. Youst and Seaburg, 51.
12. R. Scott Byram, "Colonial Power and Indigenous Justice," *Oregon Historical Quarterly* (Fall 2008): 361. The Yaquina people originally controlled the Yaquina watershed from the Yaquina River's lower bay to over thirty miles upriver. Most of their permanent living sites were located on the lower bay. Their population had dwindled from about 700 in 1830 to less than 80 by 1850.
13. Hoop, 69.
14. Youst and Seaburg, 55.
15. Ibid., 57.
16. Philip H. Sheridan, *Personal Memoirs of P.H. Sheridan* (New York: Charles L. Webster, 1888), 99.
17. Ibid.
18. Hoop, 56.
19. Youst and Seaburg, 57.
20. Hoop, 69.

21. Sheridan, 99-100.
22. Ibid.
23. Youst and Seaburg, 75. The depot was located about a half mile from Murray Loop near the present-day south junction of Hwy. 229 and Yasek Loop.
24. Schwartz, 167.

4
The Matriarchs and the Free Love Movement

Like the Murray side, the Crawford branch of *Murray Loop* can be traced back to an event occurring in 1808. That was the year thirty-six-year-old Hugh Crawford married twenty-year-old Mary Wilder on November 24 in Brunswick, Maine. The Crawford/Wilder marriage sparked the matriarchal line that would one day merge with the Murrays.

Between 1809 and 1827 Hugh and Mary Crawford had nine children. Nancy, one of their daughters, plays a pivotal role in shaping the legacy of *Murray Loop*. Nancy Phedora Crawford, born in 1824 in Arkright, New York, was the eighth of nine children. Mary died when Nancy was five; her father died six years later. She remained close to her siblings, taking care of her younger brother Wilder.

When Nancy turned sixteen, she began working as a live-in tutor. Only five feet tall, she often had students, young boys especially, who towered over her. One morning, according to family lore, one of these boys pressed his advantage and disrespected her. Nancy picked up a large book and whacked him so hard he fell to the floor in surprise. She put her foot on his chest and held him there until he promised to obey her and cease causing problems. The feisty young teacher made her point, and the two of them got along fine afterwards. Nancy carried that strong spirit into all aspects of her life.

Coinciding with her teaching, Nancy felt a second call pushing her to action. An earnest young woman with strong convictions, she was determined to share her religion. She went door-to-door encouraging everyone she met to embrace Christianity if they hadn't already done so.

In 1848, twenty-four-year-old Nancy met and married twenty-six-year-old Free Will Baptist circuit preacher Lester B. Starr.[1] Nancy hoped to assist her new husband in bringing converts to Christianity. The couple settled in Plainfield, New York, and the following year Nancy gave birth to a daughter they named Sarah. As the Starrs made a home for themselves, Nancy's older sister Vina came for a prolonged visit. Vina assisted during the birth of Nancy's second child, Ina, on December 29, 1849.[2]

3. Nancy/Jennie Phedora Crawford Starr Owram (1824-1907), ca. 1860.

When Nancy gave birth to Ina, her joy was tempered by sadness. Little Sarah died shortly after Ina's arrival. Four years later, in 1854, Lester Starr Jr. was born, followed by a son, Marion, who, like Sarah, also died in infancy.

Over time, Nancy's relationship with her husband disintegrated. Their home wasn't a happy one. Her dream of working in a religious partnership with Lester faded. She remained at home alone with the children while he left for days at a time to preach.

Nancy's granddaughter Alice Murray Green attributes her grandmother's discontent to Lester's neglect. Lester dined on healthy meals provided by members of his various congregations in contrast to his wife and children who went hungry at home. Granddaughter Lucy Murray Marrs believes the rift was crueler, describing an argument over one of Nancy's pregnancies when Lester tried to force her into miscarrying.[3]

Whether due to his neglect or physical abuse, Nancy believed she couldn't stay with her husband. She started looking for a way to break free of her marriage. At this point in the story, family records become ambiguous and, to some extent, intentionally misleading. Nancy left Lester, that much is certain. Although the year can't be pinpointed, she seems to have fled sometime just before or during the first years of the Civil War.

4. Vina Crawford (1819-Unk.), ca. 1860.

When the 1860 census was taken, Nancy was found living with her older unmarried sister Mary Ann Crawford, who worked as a ferry operator in Chautauqua, New York, about 250 miles west of Plainfield. Neither her daughter Ina nor son Lester is recorded on the census with Nancy.

Although family stories don't explain when Nancy left Lester, they do explain how. The story goes that Nancy wrote to a relative in Ohio asking for his help:

> Elder Starr was so cruel to her and the children that one time she wrote a letter to a relative in Ohio and had a trusted neighbor woman mail it. She asked him if he could come help her and the children escape while Elder Starr was on a trip of some duration. It was all arranged with the help of this neighbor. One night [her relative] came with horse and buggy, and [Nancy] had the children ready and just extra clothes was about all, and they took off silently so no one would know when or where [they] went and couldn't tell Elder Starr a thing when he returned. They drove as long and fast and far as they could, finally reaching [her relative's] home in Ohio.[4]

Nancy's plan worked. She and the children left without discovery. Their Ohio destination brings up some interesting possibilities later in the story. So does her relationship with one of her helpful neighbors.

50

Determined to start fresh, Nancy changed her name to Jennie. Jennie P. Starr covered her escape so well that her trail is still cold 150 years later. Little is known about how she filled her days or where she lived. Her granddaughters believed she might have supported herself and her children by teaching school or working as a seamstress in Ohio or New York. Wherever she was, she was well hidden.

Leaving her husband didn't guarantee freedom for Nancy/Jennie. She would have known that although Elder Starr was out of her life, he still dominated her future. The stringent state laws governing divorce in nineteenth-century New York gave women few options when they wanted to leave their husbands. Women could rarely sue for divorce; even a legal separation was difficult to obtain. Jennie could leave her husband, but she couldn't break the legal bond between them. Only Lester could do that.

5. *Children of Nancy and Lester Starr: Lester Milford Starr Jr. (1854-1923) and Ina Claire Starr (1849-1928), ca. 1861.*

As a rule, divorces were granted only on charges of adultery, a charge Lester later used to obtain their divorce. If a woman were so charged she was not allowed to remarry, at least not within the state of New York.[5] The inequity of the divorce laws did not stop Jennie from seeking her independence. The law might, however, have affected her view of marriage. At some point she was introduced to the free love movement.

During the 1850s, this movement had taken up the cause of women, marriage, and reform in the United States. Earnest radicals came together in a variety of communities that shared their ideas of free love, a concept that differs from a similar movement in the United States one hundred years in the future.

The phrase *free love* in the twenty-first century is often associated with sexual experimentation and the counterculture of the 1960s, but the free love movement of the 1860s did not advocate short-term sexual relationships or multiple sex partners. The nineteenth-century term referred to relationships that were freely entered into and not regulated by law or religion; free love participants usually entered long-term monogamous relationships without the legal bonds of marriage.

Proponents of the free love movement included middle-class reformers who resisted laws that prevented unmarried couples from living together and government legislation that regulated adultery and divorce. Adherents also sought freedom from church interference in personal relationships. Free love advocates believed that love growing from the natural laws of attraction would blossom to bind two people together in peace and harmony, strengthen the bond of family and home, and produce healthy, happy, loving children.[6]

Free love leaders gave speeches, authored publications, and sought to educate their audiences about the ideals they themselves acknowledged as "radical." Their ideas found support with independent-minded people who varied in philosophy from Christian fundamentalism to Darwinism. Many of the followers lived in communities across New York and Ohio where they could share their beliefs without conflict. One location seemed especially welcoming.

Of the nearly 500 communal experiments undertaken in the United States during the nineteenth century, the Berlin Heights area of Ohio stands out as a unique example of community acceptance.[7] Between 1857 and

1877 there were seven attempts to establish a utopian community at Berlin Heights.[8] As founders sought to keep these unusual communities alive, they often wrote articles expressing the group's goals and intentions. Eight different journals and/or newspapers were published in Berlin Heights over a twenty-year period. They all reflected the social reformist attitudes and strong sense of individuality that play important roles in *Murray Loop* history.

The first free love group to organize in Berlin Heights consisted of twenty members. They came together in 1856.[9] Some of them lived communally while others lived individually. All respected the ideals of personal freedom, honest commerce, women's rights, and free love.[10] Many in the group supported abolition and practiced temperance and vegetarianism.[11]

Some established families in Berlin Heights weren't ready to see the world from this new perspective, so the free love colony faced suspicion and resistance. Undaunted by their neighbors' doubts, the earnest believers overcame this early prejudice by working hard and remaining true to their ideals. Years later, after the free love colony had long been discontinued, one of the older community leaders acknowledged the positive attributes of the free love advocates once living in the area:

> As a matter of fact, the members of the community, though dreamers, were conspicuous for intelligence, industry and good citizenship. . . In their hands the waste places of the town became its garden spots. They were the pioneers in various industrial enterprises. They were quiet and law-abiding: and not least among their virtues was their capacity for thinking well of others and minding their own business.[12]

Through their integrity and contributions to community and commerce, the free love followers had overcome their neighbors' hesitation, and the two groups lived in peace.

Although the utopian colonies eventually disbanded, Berlin Heights remained a place where free love followers could go to find people who believed as they did. Over time the number of free love advocates increased. One of the newcomers, Joseph Owram, would play a pivotal role in Jennie Starr's future.

Joseph Owram grew up in Barnsley, England. A relatively small and somewhat frail child, he had three brothers and a sister. Joseph's parents wanted to ensure their sons learned a trade, so in 1840 when Joseph was fourteen, his parents apprenticed him to a tailor. For seven years Joseph spent long hours sitting cross-legged on a bench, learning to sew instead of working in the out-of-doors he loved. In 1847 he turned twenty-one and finished his apprenticeship.

Free to earn his own living, Joseph decided to immigrate to the United States. As he prepared to leave England, he packed the scissors and tools vital to his trade, including a heavy black iron.[13] The iron had a swinging door at the back so the hollow base could be filled with hot coals and emptied when the ashes cooled.

Since Joseph's father had already visited the United States at least once looking for work, Joseph had some idea of what to expect when he arrived. Little is known about Joseph's early years in the United States, since family records yield little information about how or where he lived. He married an Englishwoman named Harriet (Hattie) about 1854, and the two settled in Burlington Flats, New York, where they had two children, George and Alice.

Burlington Flats was roughly eight miles north of Plainfield, home to Nancy and Lester Starr. Both were small communities so it seems reasonable that the Starrs and Owrams knew each other. In describing Joseph and Jennie's relationship, granddaughter Alice writes that the two had met while Joseph was still married to Hattie.

Joseph Owram's history is a bit obscure between 1860 and 1866. At some point during these years he and Hattie separated, although they remained good friends. Both of them were living in Berlin Heights, Ohio, when Jennie Starr was living there, too. There aren't any records tying Joseph directly to the free love movement, but his lifestyle fits well with their beliefs. His separation and continued friendship with Hattie, his vegetarian diet, and his devotion to the abolition of slavery set him apart from many men of his time. So did his choice of residence. Joseph's idealism fit well with the goals and aims of free love. So he would have been drawn to Berlin Heights for many reasons.

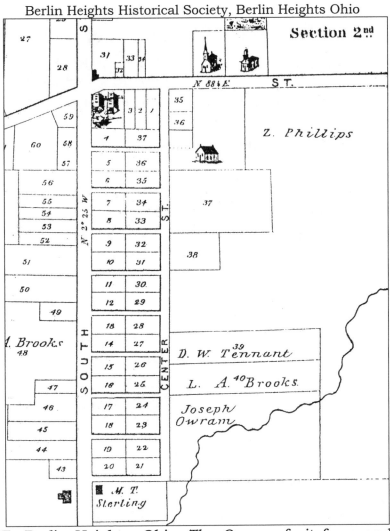

E. Berlin Heights, Ohio. The Owram fruit farm and vineyard encompassed about five acres as shown on this 1874 section map. Old Woman Creek divides the property and runs into Lake Erie about five miles to the north.

59

As for Jennie Starr, she seems to have experienced an unexpected shift in perspective. Granddaughter Lucy describes her as "very much a lady, prim, proper and restrained," shielding Jennie's reputation against the adultery charges that Lester used to get their divorce. But Jennie wasn't so simply defined. Sometime after 1860 she is living with Joseph and they are not married. The couple was settled on a fruit farm located in Berlin Heights.

In addition to its link to free love, Berlin Heights is also connected to the Underground Railroad and the struggle against slavery:

> That fugitive slaves were conducted through Berlin Heights and within yards of the buildings held by Free Lovers is beyond dispute. At least two well-to-do Berlin residents, a Mr. Brainard and O.C. Tillinghast, were instrumental in conducting slaves and in aiding them with money and teams.[14]

Joseph and Jennie seemed to have made a place for themselves alongside men like Brainard and Tillinghast. An intriguing story passed down through the family provides a clue to how strongly the Owrams supported the abolitionist cause:

60

Tall grass, bushes and shrubs grew wild in one corner of the Owram farm, an area that remained basically ill kept while all other areas of the property and fences were kept clean and immaculate. The Owrams secreted runaway slaves in a small cave hidden within this uncultured corner field. The entrance to the cave lay hidden behind some brush near a fence corner, and was kept stocked with food, water, bedding, and necessities.

The night after the runaways arrived, a "conductor," or guide, would arrive at the farm to take the escaping souls across the border into Canada.

One day, Southern slave catchers came to the Owram farm looking for fugitive runaways. One of the bounty hunters happened to notice the ill-kept corner property and asked . . . why this area lay undeveloped. The Owrams explained that they liked to nurture local birds and wildlife, so they let that one area lay fallow as a concession to nature. This seemed to satisfy the bounty hunter's question, and the men did not investigate.[15]

The story places Joseph and Jennie in Berlin Heights by 1861. The date is difficult to establish since few details of their lives during the early 1860s can be documented.[16]

In 1866, Jennie's sixteen-year-old daughter, Ina, fell in love with twenty-five-year-old Civil War veteran Hamilton Sturdevant. Jennie was opposed to their marriage because of the age difference, and because Capt. Sturdevant was inclined to heavy drinking. After a tantrum in which Ina threatened to kill herself if denied Hamilton, Jennie gave the couple her blessing, and they were married on July 4, 1866. The following year Hamilton and Ina moved to Clay County, Kansas, where they established a homestead.[17]

In 1868, forty-three-year-old Jennie was pregnant. Jennie's attending physician warned her about the risk she faced giving birth at her advanced age, but she was nonetheless pleased with her condition. By all accounts, the doctor worried for nothing. Jennie seems to have experienced a healthy pregnancy, give or take the occasional craving.

Since Joseph was a vegetarian, the family didn't keep meat on hand. One day Jennie found herself craving beef. There wasn't any at home so she walked to a neighbor's house, asked for some, and was happily obliged. Aside from this one craving, Jennie adapted to Joseph's vegetarian lifestyle. One family story relates that Jennie cut back on the amount of squash served at dinner when she noticed Joseph's skin turning orange.

On October 2, 1868, Jennie and Joseph greeted the arrival of their daughter, Minnie Alice Owram, their first and only child together. Mother and daughter were both healthy, and Minnie, the future matriarch of *Murray Loop*, quickly became the darling of the family.

The Owrams shared a peaceful routine on their Ohio fruit farm and enjoyed being active participants in the community. Joseph's first wife, Hattie, and fifteen-year-old son, George, lived nearby. Hattie was married to Edwin Winchell, a carpenter, and the two families shared a warm friendship. Minnie grew up referring to Hattie as "Aunt Hattie" with great affection.[18] On November 23, 1870, Joseph and Jennie were married.[19]

Hundreds of miles to the east, three-year-old Hugh Murray was growing up in Nova Scotia. Two thousand miles to the west, the Yaquina Tract had recently been opened to settlement by U.S. citizens, an area that Minnie and Hugh would one day settle in as adults.

6. Joseph Owram (1826-1886), Ohio, ca. 1868.

4
Notes

1. The U.S. Census of 1850 lists Lester Starr's first name as Lood.
2. Vina Crawford was an unmarried schoolteacher earning $8 a month during the five-month school year.
3. Lucy Murray Marrs, "Memoirs" (unpublished manuscript in the author's possession, 1977).
4. Alice Murray Green, "Memoirs."
5. Bill Long, "Divorce in New York II, Circa 1829," http://www.drbilllong.com/LegalHistoryII (accessed June 6, 2008).
6. John Spurlock, "The Free Love Network in America 1850 to 1860," *Journal of Social History* 21, no. 4 (Summer 1988): 765-779.
7. Berlin Heights is located forty-five miles west of Cleveland and five miles south of Lake Erie.
8. William Frederick Vartorella, *The Other "Peculiar Institution": The Free Thought and Free Love Reform Press in Ohio during Rebellion and Reconstruction, 1861-1877* (Athens, OH: Ohio University Press, 1977): xviii.
9. Hudson Tuttle, "History of Berlin Township (Erie County, Ohio)," in *History of the Firelands: Comprising Huron and Erie Counties, Ohio,"* ed. W.W. Williams

(Cleveland, OH: Press of Leader Printing Company, 1879), 475-489.

10. Spurlock, 765-779.

11. Vartorella, xviii.

12. Job Fish, "The Free Love Community," *The Firelands Pioneer* 23 (September 1925): 322-323.

13. At the time of publication, Joseph Owram's scissors were on display in the home of his great granddaughter, Nancy Green Petterson, Airlie, Oregon.

14. Rush R. Sloane, "The Underground Railroad of the Firelands," *The Firelands Pioneer*, New Series V (July 1888): 28.

15. Green, "Memoirs."

16. Sloane, 58. According to this historian, the last escape of fugitive slaves in Ohio occurred in 1861 immediately preceding President Lincoln's inauguration.

17. Lee Ann Potter and Wynell Schamel, "The Homestead Act of 1862," *Social Education* 61, no. 6 (October 1997): 359-364. The Oregon Donation Land Act expired in 1855. Pressure groups in Washington, D.C., immediately called for new land distribution legislation for undeveloped land outside of the original thirteen colonies. The Republican Party made homestead and land distribution a part of its 1860 election platform. Southern states had been opponents of the policy, but their secession from the Union cleared the way for successful legislation. The passage of the Homestead Act of 1862 became one of the most popular government programs in U.S. history. Any law-abiding citizen, male or

female, who was the head of the household, could claim 160 acres of unoccupied government land. Claimants had to "improve" the homestead by building a dwelling and growing crops. After five years, if they were still on the land, the property became theirs, free and clear. Between 1862 and 1986, ten percent of all land in the United States was claimed under the Homestead Act.

18. Green, "Memoirs."
19. Jennie Starr and Joseph Owram are listed in a book of marriages for Erie County, Ohio, in 1870.

5
The Yaquina Tract

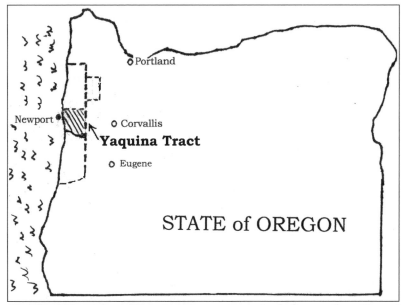

F. The Yaquina Tract was separated from the Coast Indian Reservation in 1865. The area is indicated by diagonal lines.

In 1848, the California gold rush began. The scramble for gold had an unexpected impact on the Willamette Valley. By late 1848 most of the male settlers throughout the valley went to the newly discovered gold fields of California. Many of them returned to invest their gold dust in their communities.

As thousands of gold miners arrived in California from all parts of the world, new markets opened. One of the fastest growing enterprises began with the discovery of Willapa Bay oysters north of the Columbia River during 1851. Hungry gold miners paid premium prices for the succulent seafood. The orders for these tender oysters grew quickly, creating the foundation of the oyster industry in the Northwest.

In 1852 the schooner *Juliet* wrecked near Yaquina Bay. While stranded, her captain discovered great quantities of oysters along the Yaquina River.[1] The emerging oyster market made his findings worth noting. For whatever reason, the oysters were left undisturbed. A few years later when the Coast Indian Reservation was created, the oyster beds had been all but forgotten.

By the time Oregon attained statehood in 1859, various entrepreneurs and opportunists were beginning to take notice of the resources available along the central Oregon coast. In 1861 Captain Spencer from Shoalwater Bay, Washington Territory, visited the Yaquina Bay oyster beds and saw their commercial potential. He published his ideas and set the gears of economic development in motion.[2]

In 1863, Yaquina Bay was still part of the Coast Indian Reservation when two competing oyster firms, Winant & Company and Ludlow & Company, began harvesting Yaquina Bay oysters for shipment to San Francisco. Indian Agent Ben Simpson, on behalf of the reservation, charged both companies a fee for each bushel of oysters harvested. Winant paid; Ludlow did not. Before long the two firms were fighting over oyster rights, rights that legally belonged to the tribes living on the reservation. The dispute drew considerable public attention to the Yaquina Bay area.[3]

Coinciding with the oyster confrontation on the Yaquina, business interests in the mid-Willamette Valley counties of Lane, Linn, Benton, and Polk recognized that a shorter, more direct sea route to San Francisco for Willamette Valley export might be found at Yaquina Bay. In 1863, to add weight to these interests, Agent Simpson suggested in his annual report that the Coast Reservation be reduced in size.[4] Also that year, Corvallis mayor and former Coast Indian Agent B.R. Biddle, along with James R. Bayley, Corvallis doctor and former Siletz Agency physician, and Corvallis newspaper editor T.B. Odeneal, incorporated a project known as the Corvallis and Yaquina Bay Wagon Road Company.[5] In 1864, construction was begun on the road, which was completed from Corvallis to Nortons, just outside reservation boundaries. By having access to the Yaquina harbor, the entrepreneurs reasoned that Willamette Valley farmers could ship their products more economically to San Francisco than by using the much longer, already established Columbia River route further north.

In Washington, D.C., former Oregon Indian Superintendent James Nesmith, who was a U.S. senator in 1865, lobbied for the opening of the Coast Reservation.[6] His efforts in Washington paid off. On December 21, 1865, barely ten years after the establishment of the Coast Indian Reservation, President Andrew Johnson issued a federal mandate opening the Yaquina Tract to non-Native settlement.[7] Reservation Indian leaders were not consulted; only the presidential decree was needed to take the land from the Indians.

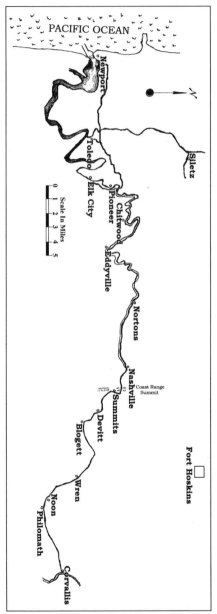

*G. Route of the Corvallis—Yaquina Bay Wagon Road,
adapted from the 1952 Metzger map.*

73

The Yaquina Tract split the reservation in two. The district included a twenty-mile east-west swath running roughly ten miles north and twenty miles south of the Yaquina Bay tributary, adding up to over 200,000 acres.[8] The northern part of the reservation became known as the Siletz Reservation. The southern part became known as the Alsea Reservation and remained under the jurisdiction of the Siletz Agency.

For Native Americans who had been living in the Yaquina Tract district, Congress made an appropriation of $16,500 to compensate them for improvements on their land that included fencing, housing, and other structures.[9] Settlers, however, began moving in before the Native Americans living in the area were removed.

On January 8, 1866, individuals who had been waiting impatiently in the Willamette Valley for the "go ahead" began moving to the Yaquina Tract.[10] Describing the frenzy of behavior, historian David D. Fagan quotes an interview with Alsea Indian Sub-Agent George Collins:

> . . . intense excitement prevailed throughout the entire Yaquina country. Every man appeared to be the possessor of a valuable secret. People were to be encountered moving up and down and

across the river. A "boom" raged. [One setter] walked into Coquelle John's hut, on Coquelle Point,(See map page 171) and with the untutored mind that the land belonged to the whites, hustled the Indian out and seated himself on a soap box by the fire. In less than an hour [another man] arrived on the scene, gave eighty dollars for his chance. [The first man] pocketed the money, jumped into his canoe and quickly had another claim where he notified all comers, "On this day I have took the present site of Newport."

In a little while those from the Willamette Valley commenced to arrive; all became mad with excitement; claims changed hands rapidly; money was plentiful; speculators ran riot.[11]

Aggressive speculators seized Native American homes and farms.[12] Within six months the incoming population between the Yaquina tidewater at Pioneer City and the coast, a distance of thirty miles, had grown to over 300.[13]

Writing an editorial for the *Corvallis Gazette*, one man visiting the area described the changes he saw taking place:

On both sides of the river, its entire length, I found settlers; each busy clearing the wilderness, building dwellings, and otherwise developing this truly fertile country.[14]

As time passed not all of those who visited came to stay. Many were tourists who began to make annual coastal trips in mid to late summer. They were seeking a cooler climate to relax and play in during the dog days of summer. Some visitors came for health reasons, taking advantage of the salty ocean breeze.[15] Malaria, known to be endemic in parts of the Willamette Valley, was not found at the coast. Before long an annual tourist trade energized the economy.

One popular destination was the north bay shore at the mouth of the Yaquina harbor where an unnamed town site was established before being dubbed Newport in July 1866. A sandstone cliff 130 feet high protected the area from blustery afternoon winds. By September, approximately twenty-six buildings had been erected there.[16]

The most prominent structure at North Beach was a hotel called the Ocean House.[17] Located on the bluff where Lt. Sheridan had built a temporary block house in 1856, the hotel had the only yard along the waterfront[18] and became a popular resort.[19]

7. *The Ocean House, Newport, Oregon, 1866. Samuel Case is leaning against the post and Dr. L.P. Baldwin, his partner in the hotel is standing on the balcony. Today the United States Coast Guard Station in Newport is located on this site.*

On July 4, 1866, the Ocean House hosted an Independence Day celebration that also recognized the opening of the Yaquina Tract. People living along the bay came to participate in the activities. Others in attendance were Indians from the reservation and people from the Willamette Valley who lived as far away as Oregon City.[20]

OCEAN HOUSE.

On the North Beach at the

MOUTH OF YAQUINA BAY.

THE SUBSCRIBER, has erected a comfortable house on the North Beach, at the Mouth of Yaquina Bay, and is now prepared to accommodate boarders and lodgers, on reasonable terms

April 7, 1866.   SAMUEL CASE

8. Corvallis Gazette, Corvallis, Oregon. July 14,1866.

The wagon road from Corvallis to Nortons had been recently extended to Elk City on the Yaquina River. Another small town named Pioneer City lay two miles further upriver at tidewater. Here Captain George Kellogg moored his cargo steamer *Pioneer,* using it to transport passengers and deliver cargo up and down the river. On July 4, Kellogg carried passengers to the celebration site at the Ocean House:

> At five o'clock in the morning the steamer *Pioneer* left her moorings at

Pioneer City [21] with about seventy-five persons on board and proceeded down the bay, touching at different points and taking on passengers. On arrival at North Beach they were loudly cheered by the crowd. . . there were assembled nearly four hundred white settlers, besides about three hundred red-men, who had come to witness the. . . new and strange procedure of the Boston men.[22]

At eleven o'clock the crowd gathered around the speaker's stand near the Ocean House where prayers were given followed by singing and four short patriotic speeches. On behalf of the ladies of Corvallis, former mayor B.R. Biddle next presented the flag to newly settled bay resident Mrs. Thorn. The flag was then raised in the midst of three cheers for the donors and nine cheers for the American flag. Sam Case read the Declaration of Independence followed by a meal served at noon.

About 350 settlers and visitors enjoyed the banquet of seafood, after which the Native Americans were invited to eat the leftovers. A saloon near the Ocean House sold alcohol; although a number of intoxicated people were observed in the crowd, a Corvallis newspaper reporter wrote that they behaved themselves.

9. *The stairway on the right led to Butch Hammer's card room and whiskey saloon; the building on the left was Livingston's Cakes and Beer Shop, Newport, Oregon, ca. 1866.*

Following lunch, former Coast Indian Reservation Agent David Newsome delivered a celebratory toast of hope and optimism:

> Benton County, the bright and rising star of Oregon. She stands central in position and with one hand extending westward along her own superior Yaquina Bay to the almost boundless Pacific Ocean, she invites the commerce of Asia and California to the bay. And from the head of tide she reaches forth her other arm along a natural line of

routs [sic] for a railroad eastward to connect the great artery of our Nation—the Pacific Railroad.[23]

Newsome's eloquence expressed the vision and wishful thinking of people throughout Benton County that Yaquina Bay would develop into one of Oregon's major seaports with Newport as "the germ of the San Francisco of Oregon."[24]

At three o'clock, landowners on the lower bay held an impromptu meeting and agreed to name the newly platted community at North Beach "Newport."[25] The celebration ended at four o'clock and people returned to their homes, happy to have celebrated the first Fourth of July on the bay.

Seven months before, on January 8, 1866, Joseph Graham and William Mackey, two of the earliest settlers, had left Corvallis for Yaquina Bay:

> Their outfit consisted of a team of horses and a wagon with a rowboat for a bed. . . At Nortons, which was at the time the end of the wagon road, they left their team and launched the boat after cutting the brush away from the banks of the river, and after many weary hours of travel, they arrived at the end of the toilsome journey.

Mr. Mackey filed a claim on the south side of the Yaquina River while Mr. Graham took the one where Toledo [would one day be] located, but being only twenty years of age he was unable to hold it so his father, John Graham, with one of his daughters, came over and took charge of the claim. A year later [Joseph] took the claim west of his father's. . .

When they first came here, there was nothing but mountains covered with old burnt snags, and the tidelands were covered [with] tules and had many dangerous tide holes into which one might fall without the least warning. . .
26

The Grahams staked their claims along the tideland where Depot Slough merged into the Yaquina River about thirteen miles upriver from the coast. Their homestead was known as Graham's Landing until 1868 when the name was changed to Toledo.[27] Recognizing the potential around him and with great expectations for the area's development, John Graham platted a town site above the tidal flats surrounding his home. But the economic incentive leading to Toledo's development as a town would have to wait almost twenty years.[28]

The nearby Depot Slough watershed held an abundance of harvestable old growth timber that had survived devastating fires the previous two decades. The natural forest growth consisted of cedar, maple, spruce, and Douglas fir. Royal A. Bensell, George Megginson, and J. S. Copeland were among the first businessmen to take advantage of this timber potential. They staked their claim near the old military depot along Depot Slough and erected the Premier Sawmill, the first steam-powered sawmill in the area.[29]

With business going well, Bensell, under the pseudonym Rialto, wrote the following article in 1866 for the *Corvallis Gazette*:

> I visited the Premier Saw Mill on the Depot Slough and found one of the best steam saw mills in the State, sawing 7 and 8 thousand feet, per day; a lumber yard containing good saleable lumber; boats coming and going, loaded with lumber all the time. This is a lively place; some 15 hands employed; the company speaks favorably of their prospects. And the Steamer Pioneer has made arrangements to stop at this place and freight lumber to all points of the Bay. Depot Slough runs through a well-timbered district.[30]

Writing as Rialto may have made Bensell sound more objective, but his tone is justly that of a promoter. The mill was a great success, so much so that a small community named Milltown sprouted for a time at the site. During the mill's off hours, the owners held dances that added to the liveliness of the place.

10. *This undated photograph is believed to be of the Premier Sawmill on Depot Slough north of Toledo, Oregon.*

Taking advantage of the Premier's tidewater location, the company transported freshly cut lumber downstream on the ebb tide, sending the lumber on seagoing vessels destined for San Francisco. For local delivery, Kellogg's boat *Pioneer* distributed lumber to all points along the Yaquina River.[31] In 1869 the mill was employing five men and working eleven hours a day filling orders.

Early in 1866 the Bay Wagon Road and Stage Line opened service between Corvallis and Elk City charging $4 a ticket.[32] The journey covered over forty-five miles and took twelve hours.[33] Passengers seeking points downriver continued their travel by river boat. Elk City prospered.

After five years of construction, the entire wagon road between Corvallis and the beach at Yaquina Bay was completed in June 1873. However, many tourists continued to use the river route as part of their excursion to the coast.[34]

Lucy F. Blue described John Graham's house in Toledo during a visit in 1873:

> We stopped at Toledo, consisting of one house a little above tidewater and owned by one of the first settlers, a Scotchman named John Graham, blessed with a large family of daughters and only one son. The Post Office was in Mr. Graham's house, and consisted of a box nailed to the wall with a few

divisions in it where the letters for the outlying ranches were placed.[35]

About 197 settlers were living in the surrounding area at the time. Further downriver, the town site of Newport boasted a year-round community of sixty.

11. John Graham's homestead on Depot Slough, Toledo, Oregon, 1884. A locomotive is shown passing behind the right side of the house.

The stage line wasn't the only business to prosper. Shipping lines were also seeing commerce. In addition to the shipments of lumber from Depot Slough, the wharf at Oysterville, located about seven miles from the lower bay, was regularly receiving and shipping goods. Businesses used the pier there to ship oysters, furs, and firewood to markets in San Francisco and Portland.[36]

While communities grew along the river, more and more ships made their way in and out of the Yaquina harbor. The channel at the mouth of the bay had an average depth of about ten feet at low tide, accommodating moderately sized ships:

> The spring tides, with the ocean in its normal condition, rise and fall nine feet. During strong west winds the high tides have reached a height of twelve feet above mean low water mark. The influence of ordinary high tides extends to Pioneer, thirty miles above the mouth of the Yaquina, the tide rising and falling from four to six feet.[37]

On September 6, 1868, the 100-ton schooner *T. Starr King* crossed the Yaquina bar to pick up lumber for Winant & Company at Oysterville. Capable of carrying 140,000 board feet of lumber, the ship was the largest vessel to cross the bar at that time, a sign of future prosperity.[38] As commerce grew along the river, the number of ships plying the waters of the Yaquina increased. Shipbuilding and maintenance became part of the local industry.

12. Yaquina Bay, Newport, Oregon, 1880.

By the mid-1870s summer tourism was steady, and the Ocean House had doubled in size. Local proprietors posted advertisements in Willamette Valley newspapers telling people how and when to visit. People brought their tents for camping. Once in Newport, tourists could continue traveling north and south along the beaches at low tide to explore the central coast. In less than ten years the Yaquina Tract had moved from infancy to childhood.

In 1870, while these changes were taking place along the central Oregon coast, Jennie and Joseph Owram were making plans of their own to visit England.

YAQUINA BAY STAGE LINE !

JAMES DIXON, PROPRIETOR.

SUMMER ARRANGEMENT.

Having purchased the line of stages running from Corvallis to Elk City, the undersigned proposes to run

FINE, COMFORTABLE COACHES,

Tri-Weekly, between those points, leaving Corvallis on

Mondays, Wednesdays, and Fridays,

and returning on alternate days.

THROUGH TICKETS TO NEWPORT

may be procured at Albany.

Passengers arriving at Albany, on the cars, can at once procure through tickets to the beach, at one of the most pleasant resorts in the State of Oregon.   J. DIXON.

13. Benton Democrat, *Corvallis, Oregon,*
October 25, 1873.

5
Notes

1. *Oregon Statesman,* April 8, 1852.
2. David D. Fagan, *History of Benton County, Oregon* (Portland: David D. Fagan, 1885), 480.
3. Ibid., 478.
4. E.A. Schwartz, *The Rogue River Indian War and Its Aftermath, 1850-1980* (Norman: University of Oklahoma Press, 1997), 176.
5. Ibid., 177.
6. Ibid., 178.
7. Lionel Youst and William R. Seaburg, *Coquelle Thompson, Athabaskan Witness: A Cultural Biography* (Norman: University of Oklahoma Press, 2002), 74.
8. Schwartz, 178.
9. Robert Kentta, interview by the author, written notes, Siletz, Oregon, December 7, 2008. The compensation money was never received in Siletz. The money was somehow mistakenly diverted to Grand Ronde. During land claim settlements in the 1940s and 50s, the money was reclaimed.
10. Fagan, 459.
11. Ibid., 479.
12. According to Siletz Tribal Historian Robert Kentta, Native Americans living in the Yaquina Tract during the settlement takeover included Alsea, Yaquina, Chetco, Lower Coquille Miluk, and Tututni.

13. Richard L. Price, *Newport Oregon 1866-1936: Portrait of a Coast Resort* (Newport, OR: Lincoln County Historical Society), 8.
14. *Corvallis Gazette,* June 9, 1866.
15. Fagan, 462.
16. *Corvallis Gazette,* July 14, 1866.
17. Today the United States Coast Guard Station is located on the site where the Ocean House stood in 1866.
18. Lucy F. Blue, "A Glimpse of Newport 75 Years Ago," *Waldport* (OR) *Record* (1949).
19. Fagan, 507, 510. The hotel was owned by Samuel Case, Dr. L.P. Baldwin, and James R. Bayley. In 1861 Case enlisted in the California Volunteers and came home with his regiment to Oregon as a sergeant. He served at the Coast Indian Reservation followed by four years employment as superintendent of farming on the Alsea section of the reservation. Bayley was a prominent physician and druggist practicing in Corvallis and Newport and served as a Benton County judge. He built the original home located on the future site of the Pacific Heritage and Maritime Museum on Bay Blvd. in Newport.
20. *Corvallis Gazette,* July 20, 1867.
21. Pioneer City was located at the head of the Yaquina River tidewater about two miles above Elk City. Laid out in 1866, the area looked promising for development, but high expectations soon failed to materialize and the site was bypassed.
22. "Celebration at Newport," *Corvallis Gazette,* July 14, 1866. The term Boston was used by

Northwest Native Americans to describe United States citizens.

23. Fagan, 488.
24. Ibid.
25. Ibid.
26. Addie Graham Papers, 1923, Lincoln County Historical Society, Newport, OR.
27. Lewis A. McArthur, *Oregon Geographic Names*, 5th ed. (Portland: Oregon Historical Society, 1982), 737.
28. The railroad from the Willamette Valley to Yaquina City, completed in 1884, passed through Toledo and led to the growth of the town.
29. Fagan, 479.
30. *Corvallis Gazette*, June 9, 1866.
31. Ibid.
32. The wagon road passed by Pioneer City two miles from Elk City. Founder of the town, Captain Kellogg, had speculated in 1866 that Pioneer City would become the transfer community between stage and boat on the journey between Willamette Valley and the coast.
33. Fagan, 481.
34. Ibid.
35. Blue, "A Glimpse of Newport."
36. *Corvallis Gazette*, August 11, 1866.
37. Fagan, 472.
38. *Corvallis Gazette*, September 12, 1868.

6
A Yorkshire Holiday, an Ohio Childhood

Over seventeen years had passed since Joseph Owram left England. He longed to see his eighty-year-old mother before she passed away. In the winter of 1870 the time seemed right for a visit, so Joseph and Jennie decided to spend six months in England rather than rest at home after a busy harvest season. The record of their vacation is a detailed letter Jennie wrote to her sister Vina in 1871. In it she describes the determination so much a part of the Owram work ethic: "We worked ourselves nearly to death to get ready and left home just tired out."[1] Jennie, Joseph, and two-year-old Minnie crossed the Atlantic headed toward a reunion. In her letter, Jennie recounts their meeting with Joseph's family:

> We were eleven days and a half going over. Landed at Liverpool in the morning and at night was at Barnsley in

Yorkshire at Joseph's brother George's. They knew that we talked of visiting them but did not know that we were on the way until we reached them. He had been absent over seventeen years, but they knew him instantly. We went on to the dear old Mother's the next day. She lived in the same little house Joseph left and she had just got word that we had come, but could not believe it and in her excitement and hurry had gone out to see if it could be true and came back to find us! Imagine the meeting.

Jennie had never met Mother Owram; her respect for her independent mother-in-law is evident in her letter to Vina:

She was eighty-one years old a few days after we reached there and has, with very little assistance, paid the rent of her house (nearly thirty dollars per year) and earned [her] own living. But it was not right for she has always worked very hard and should rest now. She had a mangle[2] that she used, but it was so hard for her that we finally persuaded her to part with it and promised her that she should not want. We had sent her a little means before, now we send more and shall while she lives. She has three sons and a daughter there, but though all the men are older and stouter than Joseph, they do not seem able to [do] more than care for their own families (with one exception and he seems to have little inclination).

This letter shows Jennie's willingness to help support her mother-in-law and Joseph's dedication to his mother's welfare.

Joseph and Jennie had planned to relax while they were traveling, but when they arrived there was much to get done. The daily chores, the shorter winter days, and the dreary weather altered their plans. Jennie shares these challenges with Vina:

But I can tell you a little of our visit. While we were getting ready, I left off writing, for I was so hurried and tired and I thought when we reached there I should have a nice rest and time to write lots of letters. I took some large pictures that have been waiting for years and my paints, thinking I should paint some, and my shell work tools to do some fine pieces of that work. But alas for human hopes, my paintings were untouched and letters unwritten. You will ask why? Well the greatest reason seemed to be I wasn't comfortable enough. In almost all the places where we visited the rooms had stone floors without carpets—little small fireplaces with grate and fenders where they burned coal. The weather was not near as cold as with us and yet the air was always so damp and penetrating that we were almost always shivering and hovering over the fire. We all of us had colds and coughs and Minnie required a great deal of nursing. So when you take all of this into account with the almost constant going about from place to place and the work we were compelled to do and remember that it was dark until eight in the morning and again a little after four at night you will not wonder that we did not write.

Despite the discomforts, the three enjoyed their time in England. Jennie writes that toward the end of their stay she grew wistful and ready to return home:

But Winter passed and Spring came and the hedge groves began to grow green and the skylark came and poured out his thrilling notes of sweetness as he soared away out of sight and our thoughts and desires flew back to our own little home and we longed to be [there].

From her description of the awakening countryside, Jennie displays her skill as a writer.

As the trio prepared for the return trip, they were delayed a month waiting for a family friend who wanted to travel with them. When everything was ready, they stepped aboard ship eager to reach home. Cool weather, however, made the voyage unpleasant. Jennie explains to Vina that once again the family was ill:

> We were a little longer on our return voyage but were not as sick. When a week out we passed some great ice burgs [sic] and they chilled the air terrible. I shivered with the cold for two days and we all took very hard colds and coughed for weeks after we reached home. I didn't know but spring would finish me. We reached home the last day of April, a month too late and yet we were in such a condition that we could do nothing of any account for weeks.

When they arrived back at the farm, weakened by illness, the family couldn't afford to rest for long. Too many loose ends remained. There were back mortgage payments totaling $800 in addition to operating costs and everyday living expenses.

Their farm in Berlin Heights lay in Erie County and Erie County was fruit country. Local crops satisfied much of the region's taste for fresh, sweet, juicy fruit.[3] The soil, well adapted for growing apples, peaches, berries, and grapes, had been deposited there thousands of years earlier by ice age glacial movement. Winds blowing off Lake Erie helped prevent devastating frosts, protecting fruit fields from overwhelming cold snaps.[4]

The diversity of fruit grown on the Owram farm was typical for the Berlin Heights area. Since the crops ripened steadily throughout the summer, the ongoing harvests allowed the family to spread out its eating and its earnings.

As Jennie recorded for Vina, strawberries were the first to ripen, and the crop was a plentiful one; the family sold seventy bushels that season. After strawberries came raspberries, currants, and gooseberries followed by blackberries. When the berries reached maturity, Joseph hired local children at two cents per quart to pick the ripe fruit. When summer waned and fall arrived, the maturing grape crop became the last harvest of the season. Jennie and Joseph hired a local woman for a dollar a day to help pick the succulent clusters. Continuing her lengthy letter to Vina, Jennie writes that they trimmed and shipped three tons of grapes to market that autumn.

Since the fruit ripened over a period of several months, the travel-weary family was able to focus on one crop at a time. Two-and-a-half-year-old Minnie helped. As the little girl worked eagerly alongside her parents, she learned not only how to choose the best berries but also the value of work. These early lessons made a place for themselves in her efficient, energetic spirit, and taught her skills she would use throughout her life.

When all the crops had been gathered and the books balanced, Joseph and Jennie found the 1871 harvest a bountiful one, allowing them to catch up on their financial obligations.

With the summer and fall behind them, the family settled into the respite between harvest and planting. In the quiet of winter they found time to recover from their trip and the demands of a busy farm. Their life returned to a more peaceful routine. Through the long winter months Joseph enjoyed playing cards with his friends. The men played together at the Owram house so often that "pass" was one of Minnie's first spoken words. During these years Joseph was leader of the Berlin Heights Band where he played a "large horned instrument."[5] Jennie kept house and, as time allowed, focused on her art.

14. Three-year-old Minnie A. Owram, Berlin Heights, Ohio, ca. 1871.

Minnie grew up watching her mother draw and paint. As the little girl grew old enough to hold a pen and handle a paintbrush, Jennie made sure her daughter learned how to mix paint, balance colors, and bring her ideas to life.

In 1881, when she was thirteen years old, Minnie and her schoolmates Alice and Celia Kilburn started "The Garland," a small hand-written magazine which Minnie illustrated. The girls' imaginations found a literary outlet in "The Garland." They wrote articles, sketched pictures, discussed local happenings, and composed poetry.

Alice Murray Green Family Collection

15. "The Garland," 1881.

Humor and rhyme were hallmarks of "The Garland." One surviving poem describes the adventures of a band of pigs. Only the last two stanzas remain in family records:

-15-
Pig number one then forward sprang.
Down dropped the gun with ringing clang.
The fisher pig brought up the rear.
Leaving the fishing pole in his fear.

-16-
That night the wise pigs in the sty,
Talked o'r their troubles with a sigh.
And with the grief they'd had that day,
They thought at home they'd better stay.

The pigs learned a valuable lesson: better the safety of their warm home rather than too much adventure away from home. *Caution* seems an important theme in the girls' poetry:

There is no love in boys,
Not even a brother.
So if girls must love,
Let them love one another.
        Mary Kilburn

When you are weary of
life's busy scenes,
go out in the garden and
hide behind the beans.
        Susan E. Winchell

There is a little flower that
grows mid many a valiant spot.
No gaudy leaves its stem adorns,
Its called Forget Me Not.
        Celia Kilburn

Neither Alice nor Lucy mentions how long
Minnie and her friends continued "The
Garland," but judging by their creativity,
they enjoyed their time as authors,
illustrators, and publishers.

Minnie blossomed with all the energy of a
healthy young girl, but maintaining a busy
farm took a toll on her parents' aging bodies.
Vulnerable to the effects of old age, achy
joints, and hard physical labor, Joseph
wanted to depend more on his tailoring skills
than on his fruit harvest to generate income.
In 1882, the family sold the Berlin Heights
farm and resettled in Clay County, Kansas,
to live near Ina and Lester Jr. The following
year, Jennie was on hand for the birth of her
son's only child, Vera Len.

Although it brought them closer to family,
the move failed to meet expectations. Joseph
was unable to generate enough business to

support the family. Within two years they were ready to leave. Their next move would take them to Liberal, Missouri, and unknowingly closer to the Murrays.

6
Notes

1. Jennie Owram to Vina Crawford, 10 September 1871.
2. A mangle is used to dry and iron laundry by passing the clothes between two heavy heated rollers.
3. Hudson Tuttle, "History of Berlin Township (Erie County, Ohio)," in *History of the Firelands: Comprising Huron and Erie Counties, Ohio,"* ed. W.W. Williams (Cleveland, OH: Press of Leader Printing Company, 1879), 475-489.
4. Ibid.
5. Alice Murray Green, "Memoirs."

7
Hugh Murray Comes of Age

Hugh Murray grew up on the family farm near Pictou, Nova Scotia. Abundant wild strawberries, raspberries, and other fruits grew nearby. During summer months, Hugh and his sisters picked the wild berries to sell in Pictou, earning a few cents for each gallon.

When Hugh reached school age he began attending classes at Sunrise School. He benefited from living close to his grandmother, Jane Murray, who often helped him with his schoolwork. Jane counseled Hugh to use proper Canadian grammar at all times. Her strict guidance was well received. Throughout his life Hugh remained critical of those who spoke slang or produced poorly written compositions. He also remained proud of the Canadian school system where he had studied. This entry from his diary shows that Hugh was an attentive student, attuned to his intuition even during his childhood:

When I first went to public school in Nova Scotia our books recorded that all our knowledge came to us through the 5 bodily senses; sight, hearing, feeling, taste and smell.

I may first prove that there is at least one more avenue that brought us enlightenment.

Occurring when I was about 11 or 12 years of age, a vivid dream of skating around our school pond found me awakening and sitting up in bed. I had no skates and knew not how to skate. I laid my disappointed head on the pillow and soon slept.

This occurred about Thanksgiving Day. Father took me to his brother-in-laws a few days ere Christmas where I always enjoyed going. There at dear. . . Aunt Nancy's I was overjoyed to let cousin Simon (two years my elder) . . . buckle his skates onto my feet and I was transformed into heaven via an erratic course and many falls, as I shuffled around on the glib ice of Big Caribou River that ran through their farm.

This dream/vision was the first that I realized another knowledge.[1]

Such premonitions are noted in family lore reaching back at least to the birth of Hugh's grandmother Jane in 1808.

Although Hugh had a likeable personality, he displayed a volatile temper. His uncontrolled anger revealed much about who he would become as an adult, but during the 1870s Hugh was just a little boy with a stubborn streak. As he grew older he liked to push his physical limits.

Desiring to succeed at whatever he did, Hugh was intensely competitive. If he and his father were clearing land, Hugh tried to move the largest rocks. If the two of them were cutting wood with a two-man cross saw, Hugh tried to out-pull his father. His strength of will knew few obstacles. David Murray took his son's spirited streak in stride, and the two worked well together.

By the time Hugh reached puberty he had survived an attack of what was probably tuberculosis and endured chronic stomach difficulty. In addition he often had "spells", moments when his heart beat so violently he believed he was dying. Nothing seemed to cure him. Hugh found his ill health frustrating, but in time he found an outlet for his frustration and an avenue for all his energy.

At fourteen Hugh discovered the fiddle. After some experimentation on his own, he studied with a local instructor. What Hugh learned at that time laid the foundation for years of pleasure. The fiddle quickly became an extension of his arm. His talent compensated for his lack of more formal training.

As Hugh's teenage years progressed his ill health continued to plague him. His parents took him to a local doctor who recommended that he eat bland food and avoid sugar, salt, spices, condiments, very hot foods, very cold foods, fried foods, coffee, tea, alcohol and tobacco. A devoted meat eater, he was grateful not to have beef, lamb, chicken, fish, and game added to the doctor's list. Hugh more or less followed these dietary suggestions throughout his life. When the doctor also recommended that Hugh might benefit from a milder climate, the Murrays took his advice.

Family records suggest that neighboring friends left Pictou and settled in Liberal, Missouri, about 1880. From Liberal they sent letters to the Murrays describing the midwestern town's unique vision of intellectualism without religion. Although nothing in the family records mentions why the unusual environment in Liberal would appeal to the Murrays, later stories may help explain the town's draw. Believing the warm summers would be good for Hugh's health, David and Lydia sold their land in Pictou and bought a place near Liberal in 1883. Life on the new Missouri farm was challenging as the family worked to reestablish themselves. David supplemented the household income by working for one of the railroads passing through Liberal.

In 1884, the Murrays' oldest daughter, Sarah, married James Albert Lightbody and moved to Maine. After studying to become a nurse, Adaline also left the family and settled in Colorado. Hugh, Simon, and Emma remained at home.

7
Notes

1. Hugh Murray, "Diary, 1945-48" (unpublished manuscript in the author's possession).

8
The Free Thinkers

George H. Walser, a proclaimed believer in self-discipline and temperance, founded Liberal, Missouri, in 1880. The small midwestern community was an experiment in intellectual living that promoted an ideal setting for free thinkers.[1] Walser defined *free thinking* as a life unrestricted by religious framework. The experiment drew many proponents. People who moved to Liberal signed an agreement not to hold religious services on their property.[2]

When the Murrays moved to Liberal in 1883, they became active participants in the unusual community. A photograph shows Hugh and his sister Emma standing with a large group in front of a meetinghouse. The handwriting on the back of the photo labels the meeting place "Harmony Hall." Research into Liberal's history didn't uncover any information about Harmony Hall but did lead to articles about a Mental Liberty Hall.[3] Mental Liberty Hall, home to classes, meetings, and performance art, played a pivotal role in the lives of Liberal's free thinkers.

16. Harmony Hall, Liberal, Missouri, 1891. Emma and Hugh Murray are in the middle row, far right.

On Sunday evenings Mental Liberty Hall opened its doors to a variety of scientists, philosophers, socialists, atheists, ministers, and priests invited to speak to the attendees. Enthusiastic crowds met weekly to join these discussions.[4] A favorite presentation included a dialogue between proponents of Darwin's recently published theory of evolution and believers in the long-established view of creationism, but any topic could be heard. Earlier in the day, classes were organized for older children who were encouraged to carry on intelligent, in-depth discussions under the supervision of teachers. These classes were often concluded with chemistry experiments.[5]

*   *   *

The Owrams moved to Liberal in the fall of 1884. They easily made a place for themselves as part of a larger group living outside the confines of mainstream thinking. Liberal's citizens bought similar magazines, argued similar ideology, and sought enlightened principles through dialogue. Members of the free love community in Berlin Heights would have been in tune with Walser's free thinking intellectuals in Liberal.

Neither Alice nor Lucy explains why either set of their grandparents chose to live in Liberal, but a case can be made that the Owrams and Murrays were following their friends and were drawn to those who thought and believed as they did. Moving to Liberal would have been a logical and expected choice for the Owrams, who believed in social reform and the need for change in the world. Less is known about the Murrays' motivation.

David Murray seems to be key to understanding the ideals and philosophy of the Murray family. Alice describes her grandfather as a "progressive socialist." Judging by the magazines David read, such as the radical socialist magazine *Appeal to Reason*, he remained interested in social reforms throughout his life. Both families shared an interest in making society healthy and safe for all people.

As she and her parents settled into their new community, Minnie brought her own sense of style to town. By the last two decades of the nineteenth century, women had started to question the necessity of corsets. The 1880s saw the establishment of the Rational Dress Society (RDS), a national organization that encouraged women to wear more practical clothing. Springing from the earlier efforts of Amelia Jenks Bloomer, the RDS believed that no woman should need to wear seven pounds of undergarments in order to compress and tweak her form into the fashionable outfits common since the 1850s. The RDS advocated boneless stays and clothing that didn't deform the body.[6] Jennie and Minnie agreed with this viewpoint and neither of them succumbed to wearing a corset.

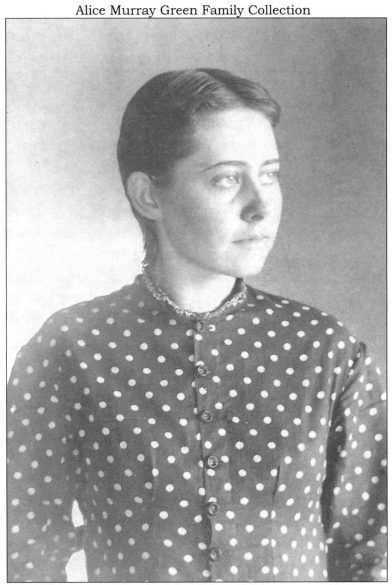

17. Sixteen-year-old Minnie A. Owram
Liberal, Missouri, 1884.[7]

As a further mark of individuality, Minnie cut her long dark tresses. Years earlier Jennie had been encouraged to do the same. Suffering from severe headaches, Jennie had consulted a physician who felt the weight of her long hair contributed to them, and he recommended she cut her hair. Recognizing the ease of her mother's style, Minnie emulated her.

Minnie's hairstyle and lack of corset weren't her only fashion statements. At times she wore a shortened skirt that exposed part of her stockings and a matching jacket that she referred to as "man-tailored." Her shoes, like Jennie's, were low heeled and wide toed for comfort. This masculine look shocked many people about town.

A newspaper reporter hearing about a "hussy" in Liberal went to Minnie's home for an interview and a picture. In his article he referred to her as an "advanced" young woman.[8] Minnie's faith in herself remained unshaken, but her nature as a peacemaker intervened. With the social opposition to her clothing, Minnie decided to modify her style. To appease those appalled by her dress lengths she started wearing leggings under her skirts. This kept her stockings covered and created less shock for anyone catching a glimpse of her legs. Compromise remained a basic part of Minnie's character, as did pleasing her mother.

In Liberal's unorthodox intellectual environment, seventeen-year-old Hugh met sixteen-year-old Minnie.

By the time Minnie moved to Liberal, she had become a talented photographer, using her camera to earn extra income for the family. Shortly after her arrival, Hugh's father asked her to photograph his farm. With her tripod, cloth covering, and powder flash she photographed the Murray house. In his diary years later, Hugh describes his father's impression of the enterprising young entrepreneur:

> I believe in that old time saying "There is a destiny that shapes our ends; rough hew them as we may". Else how explain that my father, David Murray, in Missouri was impressed by a void within that Minnie A. Owram would be my wife. She called him to peep under the dark cloth to see if her camera held the view of his house as he might best like it.

David, like his son, had a strong intuitive sense. Nearly twenty years later, Hugh Murray and Minnie Owram were married.

18. Home of David and Lydia Murray near Liberal, Missouri, 1884. Photograph by Minnie Owram.

According to family lore, Minnie's first impression of Hugh didn't lead to thoughts of a future husband. Apparently she wasn't impressed by the teenage boy.

The Owrams had lived in Liberal for less than two years when sixty-year-old Joseph suddenly died in 1886. With his passing, eighteen-year-old Minnie took over management of the family finances and support of her frail sixty-two-year-old mother. Although Jennie and Minnie stayed in close contact with their family in Kansas, they preferred to remain in Missouri and keep house by themselves.

19. Twenty-three-year-old Minnie Owram, Liberal, Missouri, 1891.

As Minnie and Jennie recovered from Joseph's death, the Murrays saw their own share of changes. Hugh Murray's grandmother Jane died in 1885. Hugh's only brother, Simon, left home to make his own way, and his sister Emma left to become a schoolteacher. Only Hugh stayed in Liberal to help his parents run the farm.

Battling the inconsistencies of farming—weather, blight, and poor seasonal markets—he tended the orchard and raised pigs. When pork prices dropped, Hugh had a difficult time finding buyers for their stock. The strawberry market, often a good cash crop, also fluctuated. Some seasons shipping costs exceeded any revenue generated by strawberry sales. Despite these ebbs and flows, the Murrays operated a well-run business. The farm, along with David Murray's supplemental income from the railroad, supported the family.

Unknown to the Murrays and Owrams at that time, the Yaquina Tract, two thousand miles away, was experiencing a boom.

8
Notes

1. *Sikeston* (MO) *Herald*, December 1, 1938.
2. *Kansas City Star*, December 22, 2001.
3. *Sikeston Herald.*
4. Brian King, "Liberal, Missouri,"
   www.spirithistory.com/81liberal.html
   (accessed December 21, 2006).
5. Steven Everly, "History of the 'Strange Town'
   of Liberal, Missouri,"
   www.angelfire.com/home/wliberalmissionout
   re/historyofliberal.html (accessed July 19,
   2009).
6. Pauline Weston Thomas, "Rational Dress
   Reform Fashion History—Mrs.Bloomer,"
   www.fashion-era.com/rational_dress.html.
   (accessed December 17, 2006).
7. About this picture of Minnie, Hugh writes in
   1946: "My Minnie, as she appeared in Fall of
   1884 when first I saw her."
8. Lucy Murray Marrs, "Memoirs."

9

"When we had to eat the seed corn, we knew it was time to move."

Between1869 and 1893 five transcontinental railroads were completed across the United States. The first passenger train service between Portland and Corvallis had been in operation for three years by the time Oregon's transcontinental connection was completed in 1883. Railroad travel greatly accelerated the number of settlers migrating west and marked the end of an era when large wagon trains took five to six months to cross the country. By rail, the trip took less than a week.

In December 1884 the Willamette Valley and Coast Railroad (WV&CRR) opened for business between Corvallis and Yaquina Bay.[1] Controlled by its mother company, Oregon Pacific Railroad, the line provided an outlet for agricultural shipments from the mid-Willamette Valley to Yaquina Bay. Mid-valley farmers anticipated lower shipping costs with the new and shorter route to the coast.

Due to a disagreement between railroad management and the city of Newport, the line was not built to that town. Instead, railroad manager Colonel Thomas Egenton Hogg established the terminus at a deep-water access four miles upriver from Newport. There he platted a town he named Yaquina City. Yaquina City soon boasted a three-story hotel on the hill above the loading docks, a newspaper, three stores, and a bank. The terminus quickly became a bustling commercial center. The warehouse was full, the docks hectic, and travelers plentiful during the summer tourist season. During its early years, the train trip from Corvallis to Yaquina City took approximately four hours. By 1885, travel by rail offered a smoother, faster ride than the twelve-hour stagecoach trip to Elk City followed by the lengthy boat ride to Newport, the grueling route just two decades earlier.[2]

FIRST CLASS		Distance from Sea Transition	Time Table No. 108 June 1, 1925	
402 Passenger	**404** Motor			
Leave Daily	Leave Daily		**STATIONS**	
12.30 PM		774.3	TO-R YAQUINA	
f12.35		772.3	OYSTERVILLE	(No Siding)
f12.42		769.4	MOODY	(No Siding)
		766.6	ALTREE	(Spur)
●12.55		765.6	TO TOLEDO	
f		762.9	BURPEE	
f 1.10		759.3	STORRS	(No Siding)
● 1.17		756.5	ELK CITY	(Spur)
f 1.25		753.8	MORRISON	(Spur)
● 1.33		750.6	CHITWOOD	
● 1.47		745.2	TO-R EDDYVILLE	
● 2.02		738.9	NORTONS	
● 2.18		733.7	TO NASHVILLE	
● 2.35		728.5	TO SUMMIT	
		727.2	CAIN	(Spur)
f 2.44		726.0	DEVITT	
● 2.52		723.2	BLODGETT	
f 2.55		722.0	ALDER	(Spur)
f 3.06		718.4	HARRIS	
		717.2	RUSSELL	(Spur)
● 3.14		715.9	WRENS	
f 3.30		710.3	NOON	(Spur)
		709.4	FLYNN	
● 3.37		708.5	TO PHILOMATH	
● 4.05	11.30 AM	703.1	TO-R CORVALLIS	
● 4.10	●11.35	702.1	CORVALLIS JCT. (W.S. Crsg.)	
f 4.19	f11.44	697.1	GRANGER	
f 4.28	f11.52 AM	692.6	NORTH ALBANY	(Spur)
		691.5	O. E. CROSSING	
● 4.35 PM	●12.01 PM	690.9	TO-R ALBANY	
			(83.4)	
Arrive Daily	Arrive Daily			
(4.05) 20.42	(0.31) 23.61		..........Time over District.......... ....Average speed per hour.........	

20. *1925 Southern Pacific timetable, Albany to Yaquina City.*[3]

Since no direct wagon road connected Yaquina City to Newport, coast-bound train travelers disembarked at Yaquina City and boarded a ferry to complete the last four miles of their journey. People didn't mind the transfer. Summertime vacationers could leave the Willamette Valley heat in the morning and reach Newport's cool resort beaches by lunchtime. Tourism blossomed.

Lincoln County Historical Society

21. Railroad depot, Toledo, Oregon, 1890.

While Newport was coming of age as a tourist destination, Toledo, thanks to its geographical location, access to river travel, and new railroad service, was developing into the commerce center for the area.[4] The town was set to become the financial, manufacturing, and market place for people engaged in lumbering, farming, dairying, growing fruit, and raising cows, sheep, goats, pigs, and poultry. By 1884, Toledo had grown to include a commercial dock, two stores, a hotel, saloon, feed stable, blacksmith's shop, school, and post office.[5]

* * * *

Drawn to the opportunities available on the Oregon coast from advertisements back East, the Starrs were ready to try their luck in a new community. In 1890, after sixteen years in Kansas, Lester Jr., Hattie, and Vera Len, their seven-year-old daughter, waved goodbye to family and boarded a train bound for the Pacific Northwest. Their final destination was Toledo, Oregon.

The Starrs arrived in Toledo during a period of change. Towns along the central coast had been part of Benton County for twenty-four years. Coastal community leaders felt hampered by their isolation from the seat of county government in Corvallis some fifty miles to the east. Because they wanted more say in their own development, they began a movement to separate from Benton County.

Although the valley's less-enlightened citizens sarcastically referred to their coastal neighbors as "clam diggers," county officials considered the remote communities along the bay a valuable resource. Nonetheless, Benton County representatives did not always take the concerns of coastal residents seriously.

When county government continued to ignore the needs of coastal towns seeking improvements, coastal leaders took action. Working quietly, community leaders lobbied the state government in Salem for separation from Benton County.[6] To the mortification of the Benton County leadership, the lobbyists were successful.

In 1893, Lincoln County was created with lands separated from Tillamook, Benton, and Polk counties. Toledo was designated the acting county seat. By a majority vote three years later, Toledo became the official seat for county government; it would remain so for the next sixty-one years.

In 1893, Lester Starr Jr. was working for the newly formed Lincoln County assessor's office in Toledo.[7] His wife, Hattie, had opened a dressmaking business in town. They invited Ina, Hamilton, Jennie, and Minnie to join them in Oregon. Despite Toledo's appeal, the Sturdevants and the Owrams weren't quite ready to move.

22. The Toledo commercial waterfront (shown here ca. 1912) was established in 1866 near the intersection of Depot Slough and the Yaquina River.

In Missouri, Jennie and Minnie were content. There are few stories written about them following Joseph's death. An 1891 photograph taken outside a private home shows Minnie standing with a Christian Science class.

23. Christian Science class, Liberal, Missouri, May 2, 1891. Twenty-three-year-old Minnie Owram is standing in the back row, fifth from the right.

By 1892, after spending eight years in Liberal, Jennie longed to be closer to Ina and Hamilton. Coinciding with Jennie's desire to see her daughter was a change in the Liberal community. Walser's secular vision was losing ground to churches and saloons. Minnie and Jennie decided to return to Clay County, Kansas, to live near Ina and Hamilton. They were well received, but times were hard.

The Sturdevants had spent twenty-five years struggling to make their Kansas homestead a success. In contrast, Lester was now sending letters describing the

132

potential of life in the Pacific Northwest. New people migrating there were helping the area grow. Newport's winter population reached over 250, while Toledo, now the county seat, had grown to 400.[8]

Thanks to the convenience of the railroad, the coastal area continued growing in popularity as a summertime tourist destination. People flocked to the coast, renting rooms and living in tent cities.

In 1895, a drought swept across the Midwest, wreaking havoc on many Kansas farms. After a devastating crop failure, the Sturdevants were fed up with farming life. Intrigued with Lester's descriptions of the beautiful area out West, the family decided to leave Kansas. They sold their property, packed their belongings and moved to Oregon. Minnie and Jennie accompanied them on the journey.

Reflecting back years later, Ina summarized her family's life in Kansas with curt precision: "When we had to eat the seed corn, we knew it was time to move."[9]

24. Ina Starr Sturdevant (pictured here ca. 1870) spent twenty-eight years as a Kansas frontier wife. The buttons on her dress were taken from her husband's Civil War uniform.

9
Notes

1 Lloyd M. Palmer, *Steam Towards the Sunset: The Railroads of Lincoln County* (Newport, OR: Lincoln County Historical Society, 1990), 8. In 1886 the WV&CRR name was dropped and the railroad was called the Oregon Pacific Railroad. In 1897 the Oregon Pacific Railroad became the Corvallis and Eastern Railroad. The name changed one more time in 1915 to the Southern Pacific Railroad.

2 David D. Fagan, *History of Benton County* (Portland, OR: David D. Fagan, 1885), 481.

3 *The Official Guide of the Railways and Steam Navigation Lines of the United States* (New York: National Railway Publication Co., October 1928).

4 Palmer, 164. From 1885 to 1928, daily passenger trains ran from Corvallis to Yaquina City. Direct railroad access from the Willamette Valley to Yaquina City made the Oregon coast a popular tourist destination. According to the July 16, 1914 edition of *Yaquina Bay News,* in 1913 over 50,000 people visited Newport, Oregon, by train, more than any other destination in the state except for Portland. The Yaquina City depot closed in 1932. In 1937 the line between Toledo and Yaquina City was abandoned.

5 Fagan, 493.

6 Robert Kentta, interview by the author, written notes, Siletz, Oregon, August 29, 2007.

7 Obituary for Lester Starr Jr., *Lincoln County Leader,* November 15, 1923.

8 *Lincoln County Leader*, July 23, 1920, and December 18, 1921. According to these newspaper records, the town of Toledo had the following populations: 1900—302; 1910—541; 1920–687; 1922–800.

9. Patricia Sturdevant Dye, interview by the author, Toledo, Oregon, September 21, 2007.

10
On the Curves of the Yaquina

Soon after arriving in Toledo, the Sturdevants bought a city lot and built a home just a five-minute walk from brother Lester's house.

For Minnie and Jennie, this first visit to Oregon was temporary. Within a year the two women returned to Liberal, where they stayed during 1896 before returning to settle permanently in Toledo the following year.[1] They arrived back in Toledo in July 1897 after a long, arduous train ride that jostled and bounced the frail seventy-three-year-old Jennie to exhaustion. Unable to walk from the depot, Jennie sat in a chair so family members could carry her uphill to Ina's house.[2]

25. *Ina and Hamilton Sturdevant in front of their Toledo home, ca. 1905. Apparently Hamilton's image has been defaced.*

Three months later, Minnie purchased a small house overlooking the curves of the Yaquina River. Located on three city lots, the Owrams' new house was a quick five-minute walk to Lester's and Ina's homes and about a ten-minute walk to Toledo's busy waterfront.

26. Minnie and Jennie Owram's home in south Toledo, 1910. The property overlooked the Yaquina River and included three city lots at the northeast corner of Seventh and Elder Street. [3] *See page 143.*

To support Jennie and herself, Minnie sold eggs from their hens as well as surplus milk and butter from their cow. The rich soil around their house produced fine vegetables and fruit and splendid flowers. Minnie sold raspberries, strawberries, and rhubarb from the garden.

The two women were frugal with both money and supplies as they worked to support themselves. They managed quite well. Like many efficient homemakers, Jennie planned carefully so as not to waste any of the food they labored so hard to provide. When canning fruit, Jennie proudly boasted that a hen couldn't survive on the trimmings she threw out. Minnie generated further income by doing odd jobs and by selling her artwork.

Yaquina Bay continued to grow as a popular tourist destination, and Minnie recognized the commercial market for her talents. Using the innovative skills she'd developed as a young girl, she briefly attempted to buy and sell books, but the venture failed when she couldn't generate adequate sales. She was successful, however, marketing her talent as an artist. Minnie fashioned beautiful, natural-looking flowers from dyed fish scales, beads, and silver wire.

In addition, she created black and white quick-portrait sketches that she called "crayon work." These sketches as well as her colorful chalk paintings sold quickly, mainly to tourists in Newport and Nye Beach.

27. *Minnie's Owram's business card, ca. 1900.*

28. *Pastel by Minnie Owram, ca. 1897.*

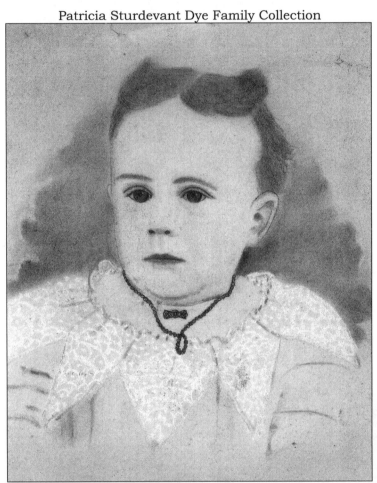

*29. Quick-portrait sketch by Minnie Owram,
ca. 1900.*

In 1900, Minnie acquired a battered and leaky rowboat that she repaired, painted, and renamed the *ENOLA*. A favorite family story plays on the rowboat's unusual name: when read backwards it spells *ALONE*.[4]

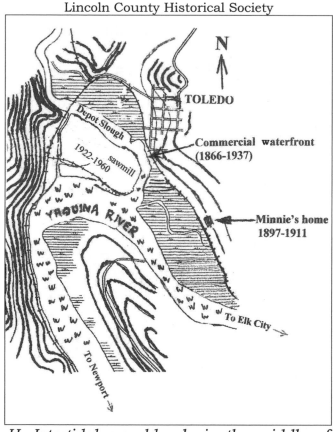

H. Intertidal marshlands in the middle of the map have been filled and are used today for industrial purposes. The map is modified from a 1923 Pacific Spruce Corporation booklet.

143

Minnie often used the *ENOLA* as both a fishing vessel and an art studio. By waiting for the correct tide, she could row rapidly up or down the Yaquina River, sketch nature scenes, and then return home when needed:

> [Mother] would row her boat from Toledo to Newport down the Yaquina River on the outgoing tide, walk up the beach to sketch scenes on little cards in pencil. . . . Later she would make these sketches much larger, and paint them with colored chalks, spray with a 'fixing' agent, so they did not smear if touched or wiped, and sell them.
>
> She loved the ocean and kept a long pole with a hook hidden at the coast. She used this to rake out crabs from the tide pools at low tide.[5]

The river's beauty provided Minnie with inspiration, nurturing her artistic talents.

30. Minnie Owram's pastel of Boone Slough, located on the Yaquina four miles downriver from Toledo, ca. 1900.

31. Boone Slough as it appeared in 2007.

In 1902 with an eye to the future, Minnie staked a homestead claim twenty-five miles south of Toledo along Drift Creek near Alsea Bay. In five years the property would be hers if she could keep up the improvements and stay on the land the required time.

Minnie's life had developed into a comfortable, creative routine when, at thirty-four years of age, she received an unexpected letter from a former neighbor.

32. This picture was on the cover of a 1903 Corvallis & Eastern Railroad Co. promotional booklet (not Minnie Owram's artwork). That year a weekend round-trip rail ticket from Portland to Newport cost $3.

10
Notes

1. Obituary for Jennie P. Owram, *Lincoln County Leader,* May 3, 1907.
2. "Local Notes," *Lincoln County Leader,* July 27, 1897.
3. Warranty Deed recorded L-406, October 30, 1897, Lincoln County Courthouse Records, Newport, OR.
4. The reflected letters L and E would have appeared backward in the water.
5. Lucy Murray Marrs, "Memoirs."

11
From "Misery" to Marriage

Hugh Murray was a lonesome man. He was loyal to his parents, but like his brother and sisters before him, he was ready to move on. Living in Liberal, Missouri, hadn't solved Hugh's chronic health problems either. His indigestion continued to cause him trouble, and he experienced bouts of malaria. Years later with tongue-in-cheek humor, Hugh referred to this time in Missouri as life in "Liberal, Misery."

In 1902, Hugh took advantage of an opportunity to earn some extra money. He drove a team of Mexican pack donkeys through the prairies of western Kansas and up the Arkansas River Valley where he sold the donkeys to a sod-house rancher. The adventure took him away from home for several weeks and, according to his diary, the awe-inspiring wild country left a deep impression.

33. Twenty-five-year-old Hugh Murray, Liberal, Missouri, 1892.

Hugh hadn't found a life's companion among the women in Liberal. He was lonesome and wanted to start a family. In 1903, he thought of his long-time acquaintance Minnie Owram living in Oregon. Remembering the vibrant Minnie

150

and his father's premonition years earlier that she would one day be Hugh's wife, he decided to write to her. Hugh was pleased when he received her response.

Hugh and Minnie shared a love of good poetry and uplifting prose. The two also shared similar views on politics and social reform. During their correspondence Hugh offered to loan Minnie some of his books: volumes of Sir Walter Scott, John Ruskin, John Keats, H.G. Wells, Longfellow, and other famous writers. Minnie accepted.[1]

34. *Thirty-year-old Minnie Owram, Toledo, Oregon, ca. 1898.*

Hugh courted Minnie with subtlety. During his early correspondence he encouraged her to look for a good man to marry. His diary shows that he didn't like her response:

> When I wrote to [Minnie] from Missouri in 1903 or 04 of the wedding of sister Adaline [to] Anthony Nelson, I expressed the hope that she too might wed some good kind man. She replied that she would not marry while her feeble old mother lived. Even then this reply struck me as a wrong attitude toward marriage, as a true husband would be glad to help . . . [and] give her old mother a much better home than [her] weak mother would [be] provided while [Minnie was] unwed. She was fated to suffer for her false outlook on life.

Although Hugh disagreed, Minnie was firm in her view that duty to her mother took precedence over marriage. Hugh was undaunted. Soon his letters took a different tone, turning more overtly to courtship. He began composing poems dedicated to Minnie that he inserted with the letters.

As the couple shared their ideas in writing, Hugh became convinced that he had found the companion he had been seeking, and Minnie basked in his regard. When the two knew that they were in love, Hugh reminded Minnie of his ill health, informing her that he didn't expect to live a long life. Minnie disagreed. She believed his health would benefit from Oregon's mild climate and invited him to join her. Hugh did not hesitate and the couple made plans to marry.

When Hugh arrived in late September 1905, he was physically depleted and tired from the trip. Minnie assisted him on the uphill walk from the train depot to her home. Among his belongings, Hugh had brought his violin, his book collection, and several fertile White Wyandotte hen eggs. Minnie quickly found a sitting hen for the eggs and thus Hugh introduced a new breed of chickens to the Toledo area.

While Hugh settled in, he visited with Jennie and immediately found an ally in his future mother-in-law. As they talked Jennie expressed her worries that she would not live to see the day her daughter married. Jennie's prayers that Minnie would find a companion were answered with Hugh's arrival.

Witnessed by a feeble but proud Jennie, Minnie and Hugh were married on September 27, 1905, by a justice of the peace. The ceremony chosen by Minnie reflected the legacy of her parents. As a child in Berlin Heights she grew up in a family not bound by the rules of organized religion. So Minnie was happy with the legal ties of a civil ceremony.

A write-up in the *Lincoln County Leader* announced the wedding:

Married

At the residence of G.R. Schenck in Toledo, Or. Wednesday evening, September 27, 1905. Miss Minnie Alice Owram of Toledo, Or. to Mr. Hugh Murray of Barton County, Missouri, Justice Schenck officiating.

The contracting parties were neighbors years ago back in Missouri, but have not met for eight years, during which time the bride has been a resident of Toledo where she is held in the highest esteem by every acquaintance.[2]

The ceremony was quiet and unassuming but nonetheless joyful. With their marriage, a new branch of the Murray clan began.

Almost immediately Hugh began to supplement the household income with his work as a music teacher. In the weeks following their wedding he placed an advertisement in the *Lincoln County Leader.*

Learn to Play

I am prepared to give instructions on the violin, guitar, banjo or mandolin. Charges very reasonable.

Hugh Murray, Toledo, Oregon.[3]

Soon the name Hugh Murray was known throughout the small community. During the following thirty-five years, Hugh encouraged and taught dozens of young people to play the violin:

> Hugh played almost any stringed instrument. He could read music and play by ear. He could delight children by holding them on his knee, giving them the bow and having them draw the bow back and forth across the strings while he fingered the notes and rotated the violin around to catch the bow movement at the right time and place, causing beautiful music to come forth. These children were so proud that they had played a violin![4]

Sometimes music lessons were taught for free and at other times there was a modest fee.

35. Thirty-nine-year-old Hugh Murray, Toledo, Oregon, 1906.

As the newlyweds began life together, Hugh was content with his new role as husband. Aside from leaving "Liberal, Misery," little in his daily routine changed as his health improved. Minnie, however, experienced more challenges in her new role as wife.

Hugh had strong views about Minnie's behavior and appearance. Whereas before Minnie had kept her hair short, now Hugh asked her to let her hair grow long. She agreed to his request. Hugh also had strong opinions about Minnie's homestead claim on Drift Creek, as their daughter Lucy relates in her memoirs:

> Mom had taken up homestead and built a little cabin to stay in up Drift Creek away from Toledo, and had only about one year more to prove up on it when Dad arrived. He would not let her go up there and stay part time (all that was required) until it was hers. So she lost it and the money it would have brought not only to her then, but to Dad also.

Minnie didn't keep a journal, at least not one that survived, so there isn't any way to know how she felt about this decision. But it is difficult to conceive that such an independent spirit didn't challenge her husband's judgment. Nonetheless, Minnie was a peacemaker.

Hugh's high-handed control extended to Minnie's friends as well, whom he discouraged from visiting during the first year of marriage. Minnie must have struggled with the loss of her freedom. Soon after the wedding thirty-eight-year-old Minnie became pregnant. Just the thought of starting a family brought her great joy. Although she had remained single to care for her mother, she had dreamed of having children and planned how she would behave as a mother. While Minnie shared a close bond with Jennie, she wanted a more relaxed closeness with her own children, a dream that stemmed from an early childhood experience.

As a young girl Minnie had once light-heartedly called her mother "Mommity" in a moment of excitement. The reserved and proper Jennie promptly chastened her for what she considered a lack of respect. Minnie decided then and there that when she grew up and had children of her own she would encourage open affection with them. Now that her opportunity had arrived, Minnie looked forward to nurturing that playful bond she'd dreamed about years earlier.

On June 22, 1906, a healthy David Joseph Murray was born at Hugh and Minnie's home. Toledo's new physician, Dr. R.D. Burgess, delivered the baby.

36. Dr. R.D. Burgess, 1922.

Named for both of his grandfathers, David's name continued a Murray tradition. For generations the Murrays had passed down the paternal grandfather's name to the first-born son. Hugh Murray, born in 1790, named his first-born son David in 1838. David in turn named his first-born son Hugh in 1867. Hugh then named his first-born son David in 1906. Little David

Murray continued an extended link with family tradition.

37. Minnie Murray and three-month-old David, September 1906.

During the first few months following David's birth, Hugh took over the household chores. He cleaned house, tended the sitting hens, milked the cow, worked in the garden, and gathered firewood.

Hugh writes in his diary how within a week of David's birth he felt an inexplicable urge to blow on his son's navel:

When son David Joseph was nearly a week in the world, I was moved to breathe upon his navel. It seems a silly impulse, but a strong one. So, new mother Minnie unwrapped his bellyband and I bent over him to breathe on the navel. But the stench of the rotting navel string was so rank that I forgot about breathing upon it. So I set to washing it with Pure Castile Soap with no salves on the cloth.

If the navel had not been covered with "gooey" dopes, it could have dried away as in all young animals in open air and sunshine. Mother Minnie had no experience with babes then.

Hugh's impulse was timely for little David, and the baby recovered quickly.

Seven months later Minnie found herself once again with child. She was excited to have a second baby on the way. Minnie was three months into the pregnancy when her experience turned bittersweet. Jennie died at the age of eighty-two. Widowed for twenty-one years, the feeble woman had lived long enough to see her fondest wish occur: her youngest daughter settled with a family of her own. Ina, Lester, and Minnie were on hand to bid their beloved mother a sad final farewell.

The *Lincoln County Leader* printed the news of Jennie's passing:

Died

At her home in Toledo, Or., April 26, 1907, Mrs. Jennie P. Owram, aged 82 years, 6 months and 2 days.

Deceased was born at Arkwright, Chautauqua County, N.Y., October 24, 1824. In 1867 she removed to Ohio, where she resided until 1882, when she went to Clay County, Kansas. After a residence of two years in that place she went to Liberal, Mo., where she remained eight years and returned to Clay County, Kansas in 1892. From that place she came to Toledo, Oregon in 1895, returned to Liberal, Mo., in 1896 on account of impaired health, and again came to Toledo the next year, where she continued to reside until her death.

She was laid to rest in Toledo Cemetery April 27, the funeral service being conducted by Rev. E.E. Rorick.[5]

Jennie's newspaper obituary helps trace the family's early history, carefully omitting the missing years when she was Nancy Starr.

*38. Jennie Owram's grave marker, Toledo Cemetery,
2006.*

The months following Jennie's burial left
Minnie mourning her loss while yearning for
her child's safe arrival. Six months later
Minnie gave birth to a healthy baby girl.
Alice Phedora Murray was born November
11, 1907. Dr. Burgess again presided over
the home delivery, charging $5 for his
services. Minnie's house on the hill was
quickly filling with a growing family.

164

39. Minnie and Hugh Murray with eighteen-month-old Alice, Toledo, Oregon, 1909.

Hugh and Minnie were busy with their growing family when in 1909 Hugh's parents sold their farm in Missouri. Hugh's younger sister Adaline wanted to care for their seventy-three-year-old mother, Lydia, at her home in Nebraska. Hugh's seventy-one-year-old father, David, wanted to contribute his skills and experience to Hugh's family in Oregon. So Lydia moved to Nebraska to live with the Nelsons while Hugh's father moved to Toledo to live with the Murrays. Hugh and Minnie were happy to welcome David.

Within a year Hugh's unmarried brother and sister also moved to the Toledo area. Simon found work constructing county roads while Emma taught school in Siletz.

By 1910, Toledo had a population close to 800, and within a five-mile radius the population exceeded 2000. Residents countywide were full of optimism and encouraged more settlers to come and make their home in Lincoln County.

40. David Murray with his three-year-old grandson David, Toledo, Oregon, 1909. In her memoirs, Alice refers to her grandfather as a "progressive socialist thinker."

As Grandfather David settled into his new life, Hugh and Minnie prepared for the arrival of their third child. On March 7, 1910, forty-two-year-old Minnie safely delivered an energetic baby girl at home. With Lucy Margaret Murray's arrival, Hugh and Minnie's family was complete. In the months following Lucy's birth everyone in the household was healthy, including Hugh who had experienced so much ill health throughout his life. With an eye to their growing family, the Murrays turned their thoughts to the future.

Minnie and Hugh decided to sell their house and three lots in town and search for a farm in the country. They quickly found a fruit farm for sale three miles north of Toledo along the east side of Depot Slough. The asking price: $1450. With a little financial help from Simon, Hugh and Minnie bought the property and prepared to move to the Depot Slough Valley.[6]

41. The Murray family standing between their garden and their house in Toledo, Oregon, 1910. Grandfather David is in the left background, with David in front of him, Hugh holding Lucy, and Minnie holding Alice.

The forty-acre farm included an established pear orchard with over forty Bartlett pear trees (among other varieties). The land included adjoining tideland flats with potential as grazing fields and cropland. Considering Hugh and Minnie's background in fruit farming, the orchard's potential must have pleased them.

11
Notes

1. Alice Murray Green, "Memoirs."
2. "Married," *Lincoln County Leader,* October 6, 1905.
3. "Learn to Play," *Lincoln County Leader,* October 13, 1905.
4. Elmo StClair, in a telephone interview by the author on June 12, 2006, also recalled an incident from 1933: "When I was in the seventh grade, Mr. Murray called me and my older brother Alton down to his place. He gave us a fiddle and got us started by showing the basics on how to run the fiddle. Alton practiced in his free time and got pretty good at it."
5. Obituary for Jennie P. Owram, *Lincoln County Leader,* May 3, 1907.
6. Lincoln County Courthouse Records, April 1911. Simon initially lived with his sister Emma near Siletz. In 1911 he bought forty acres bordering Hugh and Minnie's place on the north side. But Simon didn't like farming and later sold his place.

12
A Farm of Their Own

Scott Pirie
Collection

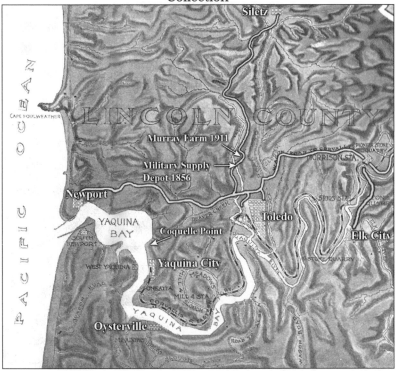

I. Yaquina Bay and River showing early landmarks. The map is modified from a promotional booklet published by Sunset Magazine, *1911.*

On April 8, 1911, Hugh hired a team and wagon to move the family and its belongings to the Murrays' new home. Simon, who was working with a road-building crew near Siletz, came to help. The new road connecting Toledo to Siletz was being graveled and provided a pleasant ride as it wound its way up the Depot Slough towards Siletz. [1]

42. *This photograph, taken during the spring of 1911, shows the newly completed hard surface road from Toledo to the Siletz River, a distance of nine miles. Hugh's younger brother, Simon, worked on its construction. Today the road is divided into a number of sections, one of which is called Murray Loop.*

As the Murrays walked the three miles to their new home, four-and-a-half-year-old David attempted to drive the family cow. When Simon saw his young nephew struggling, he put him in the wagon with three-year-old Alice and one-year-old Lucy and then herded the cow himself. When they finally reached the hill below their new home, the children climbed out of the wagon and everyone walked the final grade to the farmhouse.

A rare light snowfall greeted them.

The farmhouse, unfinished both inside and out, lacked many of the basic amenities that we take for granted today. The bare walls did not have insulation, allowing fog and dampness to seep in during cool, moist nights. As everyone unloaded the wagon and started placing furniture, Hugh and Minnie realized they were facing more than a few heating challenges as the temperature dropped.

43. Murray farmhouse, 1913. Pictured left to right: David, Alice, Lucy, and Minnie Murray.

44. Murray farmhouse as it looked in 2009.[2]

During the first night, baby Lucy, young David, and their grandfather slept in the downstairs bedroom while Minnie, Hugh, and Alice slept in the room upstairs. Bundled up, Lucy slept soundly, but in the cold, little David tossed about in his sleep. Hugh heard his son's distress from the bedroom upstairs:

> David could not bear such drafts, and sneezed and coughed until he awoke and began to whimper. I being sleepless except for brief naps past midnight, heard him and carried him upstairs and put him in my bed. . . no more sneezing nor coughing troubled our little boy.[3]

With summer soon approaching, work on the house had to wait as Hugh, Minnie, and Grandfather David expanded the orchard and planted the garden. Having brought their laying hens, milk cow, and canned food, they had the means to provide for themselves as they waited for their first harvest.

As soon as weather permitted, Hugh went to work on the orchard since it required immediate preparation in order to produce long-term yields. Hugh and Minnie wanted to ensure a varied and extended harvest that matured over several months, thus sustaining the earning potential of the farm. To do this Hugh immediately planted two fall or winter pear trees, Bosc and D'Anjou (both French varieties). He added several Yellow Transparent apple trees, sweet cherries, pie cherries, four varieties of sweet apples, Italian and French petite prunes, and two peach trees. To Hugh's eventual disappointment the peaches didn't do well. The trees produced only one nice harvest over the years.

While the Murrays expanded their crop variety, the farm that had originally been a pear orchard was transformed to apples. The new apple orchard included:

Winter Banana	Northern Spy
Baldwins	Whitney
Duchess of Oldenberg	Crabapple
Bellfloeur	Spitzenburg
Rambo	Astrachans
King of Tomplins Co.	Lady Apple
Yellow Waxen	Gravensteins

When the apple trees produced, Hugh was satisfied that their efforts had paid off.

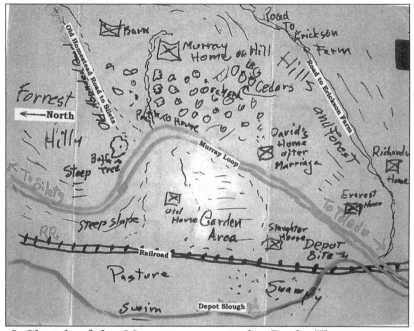

J. Sketch of the Murray property by Rudy Thompson, 2008.

Just as Minnie had done as a child, David, Alice, and Lucy learned to watch the maturing harvest to know when to begin picking. Early premature fruit on two Striped Astrachans started around July 4. The apples were tart and best eaten as soon as the fruit turned yellow. The Yellow Transparent apple trees produced handsome fruit to sell in July and August.

Alice and David helped their father pick apples, some for immediate sale and some for winter storage. Once picked, the apples were placed either under the house or in the

177

woodshed to keep cool. Stored apples could last through to the following March and occasionally hold until June. Hugh once held back a handful of Northern Spies just to see how long they would remain edible. The following year on July 4 they were still in perfect condition.[4] As the apples ripened, other crops reached maturity in succession.

From April to June rhubarb sold well at five cents a pound. Enriched with manure, the soil produced rhubarb stalks as large and long as a small adult's arm. Plantings of Gold Dollar and Oregon strawberries furnished cash crops in May and June. Red sour cherries, which did well despite raids by birds, ripened in late June. July and August brought popular raspberry crops, both Cuthbert and Black Cap. Loganberries and assorted blackberries grew and sold quickly. The French pear trees bore sweet juicy fruit that ripened during November and December. The family stayed busy planting, harvesting, canning, and selling their crops.

During their first year on the farm, Hugh eventually began work on the house, with the kitchen receiving the first change. Grandfather David, who had some savings, bought a new wood-burning cook range. The oven had a heat indicator on the door for accurate baking. There was a warming oven above the back of the stove and off to one side a tank for heating water. The range also served as the main heat source for the house. Since heat rises, warmth from the woodstove kept the upstairs drier than the downstairs. The downstairs gradually became warmer as cracks in the walls were sealed by Minnie's wallpapering.

Days filled with labor ended in the kitchen. During cold weather, family members clustered around the open door of the kitchen stove to warm their feet by its fire. Grandfather David sat on one side of the stove while Minnie settled on the other side. Hugh rested in front, sitting in a large handmade chair a neighbor had fashioned out of small whips of wood. During these quiet evenings the children enjoyed sitting on their father's lap, playing with his long hair. Lucy especially liked to comb, braid, and fuss with it.

The children joined in when Hugh sang hymns and other old songs. Sometimes one of the adults would read a serial story from a magazine. Books were also popular reading. Thanks to their parents' love of books, the children were exposed to a broad range of literature at home and often received books for birthdays and Christmas.

Swiss Family Robinson, The Thousand and One Nights, The Adventures of Sherlock Holmes, and other classic titles became family favorites. The children read these books over and over and kept them for many years.

With the new cook stove, the Murrays' most immediate needs were met. Other parts of the house saw little change. The farm's previous owner, a bachelor, ruined the downstairs floor by walking across the unprotected wood in his caulk boots. The spikes had punched holes in the floorboards, marring the wood. Hugh never repaired these floors. After a few years he laid linoleum in the kitchen, which improved the floor's appearance and simplified cleaning.

The rough-hewed farmhouse always lacked running water, nor did the farm have a hand pump. Minnie did the best she could with what was available. Two brooks on the property supplied the family's water needs. Hugh often talked about the convenience of indoor plumbing but never dedicated the money nor sought the help necessary to install water pipes that could have led from the springs at the rear of the property. From the day they moved in, Alice and David were assigned the task of carrying pails of water to the house. Since David was bigger and stronger than Alice, he carried the larger pails. Through the years the children carried thousands of pails of water for drinking, cooking, cleaning, and washing.

Grandfather David watched his daughter-in-law work hard to keep the family clean and healthy. He soon found another opportunity to improve the household by purchasing a hand-operated washing machine. The washer was quite an upgrade from the tub and washboard Minnie had been using. Grandfather David operated the new machine until the children were tall enough to push the wooden handle to and fro to agitate the clothes. A busy Minnie appreciated his help.

Grandfather David's skills benefited everyone. His ability to build simple tools helped the children work more efficiently. For example, young David, Alice, and Lucy were responsible for gathering hay, but the farm rakes were too big for them. Grandfather crafted three wooden rakes in different lengths for the children. The unique sizes fit the young farmhands and made gathering hay easier.

Grandfather sharpened all the scythes, axes, and hoes. The scythes were used to cut tall grass in hard-to-reach places. Of all the blades, the long curved blade of the scythe took the longest time to sharpen. Alice often helped. To make this job more comfortable, Grandfather set the grindstone up under an apple tree, protected from the hot summer sun. As he manipulated the blade, Alice turned the grindstone until her arms ached. Although the work was hard, Alice never complained. The satisfaction she felt working beside her grandfather offset her discomfort.

While Hugh tended the fields, Minnie took care of the vegetable garden located by the tidelands. She also stayed busy making the most of any surplus crops. Minnie canned jars of pears, assorted berries, prunes, and more, all of which the family ate until the early Gold Dollar strawberries ripened in May. Root vegetables were either left in the cool ground until needed or stored in the cellar in preparation for the winter months when the farm was quiet.

The forty-acre farm proved to be everything Minnie and Hugh sought. The soil produced good harvests and the tideland gave the children room to play and grow. Through hard work and attention to the seasons, the Murrays became self-sustaining.

12
Notes

1. Today the old meandering road is divided into four sections: Western Loop, Yasek Loop, Murray Loop, and Hudson Loop.
2. Christine M. Worman bought the Murray farm in 1972. She made the following comments in an interview by the author on April 8, 2009: "I really love this place; it's perfect, with its view and vintage charm. David Murray, who lived in the house at the bottom of the hill, introduced himself the first day we moved in. I liked him from the start- he was very helpful. We didn't know anything about country life, and he had advice on pretty much everything. Unfortunately, Dave perished in a house fire on July 12, 1982. That was truly one of the worst days of my life; it was like losing a member of the family. Many friends and neighbors who really knew Dave share the same sentiments. To this day, we still miss his stories, fiddle playing and advice. During a recent remodel, I often wondered what advice Dave would have given. Several contractors over the years recommended tearing the old house down and starting from scratch. Instead, I decided to go forward with a major remodel. When the project began in 2007, we were very pleased to discover just how well the house was built. Our contractor commented that the structure

was built like a fortress and had held up very well considering its age. Even with a complete renovation, the integrity of this old farmhouse has been maintained."

3. Hugh Murray, "Diary, 1945-48."
4. Christine M. Worman told the author that while visiting the old farm in 1988, Alice discovered that although a favorite old Gravenstein had blown over during the winter of 1978, she was delighted to find that some of the Murray apple trees were still bearing fruit.

13
"Just send word and I will come."

The Murray farm straddled the old Siletz military trail built in 1856. Although no traces of the depot remained, Rudy Thompson remembered that it had been located about a half mile south of the Murray property:

> At the bottom of the hill, right where the road made a sharp turn below their house, you can see the remains of an old road that starts up the hill. That was the remains of the old military road that went to the Siletz Indian Reservation. It went on into the hills and followed the ridges rather than the valley in order to avoid the swamps and waterways along the valley. It eventually came out and hit the current road not too far south of Camp 12.

Every Memorial Day Siletz Indian women used the old trail to visit the Murray farm to pick and fill their baskets with snowball flowers. The bushes had been planted years earlier near the rear of the house. The women gathered the clusters of beautiful white flowers to decorate their family graves on Government Hill in Siletz. They often returned to give Hugh and Minnie beautifully fashioned baskets as "thank you" gifts.

The Murrays had other contacts with their Siletz neighbors. Lucy writes about one of these visitors in her memoirs:

> An elderly Siletz Indian named Mr. Collins used to hike from Siletz to Toledo for supplies; stopping overnight both ways at our place to rest and gladly accept the simple fare, which was gladly given.
>
> Dad often gave Siletz Indians fruit and vegetables, and in turn, they gave him smoked salmon, fresh fish, even eels—whatever they had.

The location of the Murray farm between Toledo and Siletz was convenient for these neighborly interactions.

As a welcoming gift to new families in the area, Hugh would send David, Alice, and Lucy with gunnysacks full of seasonal fruits and vegetables. For neighbors who had difficulty putting down their sick or dying animals, Hugh let them know he would do the difficult job for them using his .22 rifle. Lucy recalled him saying, "Just send word and I will come."

Each year when spring gave way to summer, the whole family looked forward to eating new potatoes for Hugh's birthday on June 18 and cherry pie for David's birthday on June 27. The seasonal food bound the family to the land. As the seasons changed, so did the rhythm of the farm. Lamb, fresh butter, berries, and vegetables were the principal products during summer. Apples, pears, and cider sold well in autumn.

From December through February no grass grew for the cows to eat, so they received hay three times a day. Surplus apples, pears, and clean vegetable scraps also helped satisfy the cows' hunger. The culled fruit lowered the cost of maintaining the herd. As Alice recollects in her memoirs, for the youngest cows there was an occasional treat:

> A young cow never lost her love for a pail of warm freshly separated milk. So when there was a surplus, we set half a pail of milk before this "big baby" and she happily emptied the pail.

Alice also writes that each year Hugh raised two or three pigs, and the children enjoyed helping:

> Oh, those friendly little piglets at eight to ten weeks. At first they grew so rapidly on their four to five feedings per day. We children made pets of them, feeding them their favorite weeds and surplus fruit and vegetables.

The pigs were mostly for home use and grew rapidly on warm, freshly skimmed milk mixed with boiled discarded potatoes. When the sweet apples ripened, the pigs ate the rich leftovers. They liked ripe pears too, but could tire of them, preferring the apples.

When the animals were ready for slaughter, everyone participated. After Hugh killed the pigs, the children scalded the bodies before scraping off the bristles. When Hugh slaughtered the sheep, Alice and Lucy removed the hides, working carefully to avoid making a bad cut. Hugh was strict and demanded the girls work with precision, as a hide with a slash sold for little.

When the animals were butchered for home use, Minnie either salted or canned the meat, whichever suited the cuts best. She also prepared pork sausages and steaks that were stored in crocks and covered with melted lard. Minnie smoked and salted ham, but the ham often deteriorated in the damp, mild coastal climate. In the winter and spring these meats made delicious meals. As David got older Hugh taught him how to do the slaughtering, after which Hugh would butcher the carcass. When the children were old enough, Hugh taught them how to cut the meat for storage and cooking. The family used the liver, heart, and neck for their own meals. Hugh ate the brains and edible head parts that the children were more than happy to leave for him. What the Murrays didn't set aside for use at home they prepared for market.

One of the exceptional characteristics of the Murray family was its entrepreneurial skill. The family was constantly finding new ways to bring in extra cash, motivated by a strong work ethic.

45. *Abbey Hotel, on the waterfront, Newport, Oregon, ca. 1912. The building burned down in 1964.*

Hugh had a sales route he followed during the busy summer tourist trade in Newport. He sold produce and meat to boarding houses and private homes in Newport and Nye Beach. According to Lucy, his sales were steady starting in June:

> The old Abbey Hotel on the Newport waterfront and the Gilmore Hotel on a promontory by Nye Beach took much of the produce. Mrs. Damon who ran a boarding house in Newport was one of his very best customers. Dad also peddled to many individuals around Toledo and Newport.

People liked Hugh and depended on his lamb, pork, rhubarb, butter, new potatoes, fruit, and other produce.

The family worked hard to keep its customers happy, providing quality produce and tender meats. Lucy explains in her memoirs that during the summer Hugh made two delivery trips to Newport each week, transporting his stock in an old wagon originally used as a hearse:

> Father had a horse and buggy to peddle out the produce raised on the farm. He butchered sheep and lambs and calves, and occasionally hogs and prepared the meat for sale. After the Bateman Funeral Home had graduated from horse drawn hearses to automobiles, they gave Hugh an old white hearse, with cast iron angel wings on each side of the wagon. There was no top on it then, and Dad proudly loaded it with produce, and peddled it out in style from the hearse for several years before the wagon lay down and quit. How Alice and I wish we had at least preserved the big cast iron wings!

On his sales days Hugh was gone from early morning to late in the day, selling and talking. Lucy and Alice rarely rode along on what was for them a long, tiring, and boring trip.

46. *This Nye Beach hotel (pictured ca. 1915), located just north of old Newport, has had three names over the years: 1913–Cliff House; 1921– Hotel Gilmore; 1986–Sylvia Beach Hotel.*

Ted W. Cox

47. Sylvia Beach Hotel, August 7, 2007.

14

"Far better for a quiet woman to milk."

Hugh believed one way to teach his children lifetime skills was to give them a stake in the family business. In 1912 he brought home an Angora billy and two nanny goats and promised the children the first offspring. By that time, mohair and sheep wool had been cash commodities in Benton County for almost forty years.[1] With their father's encouragement, six-year-old David, five-year-old Alice, and even two-year-old Lucy became goat owners. Hugh followed the same pattern with Shropshire and Hampshire sheep, bringing a few sheep home and giving the children the first offspring. The children soon learned how to care for their growing herds.

48. *Herd of sheared Angora goats from a Lincoln County promotional pamphlet, 1911.*

When the animals needed shearing or their hooves trimming, the children helped their father. While David and Alice were little, their job was to turn the handle on the shearing machine. Keeping the wheel in constant motion meant aching arms, but they didn't complain. The same couldn't be said of their father.

Slow to do the shearing, Hugh had a short temper that often got the better of him. At times he was angry with the animals or with the children, yelling as he worked. When David, Alice, and Lucy grew big enough to use the shearing head safely by themselves, they took over the job completely, preferring to do the work in peace.

The children were responsible for the herds in other ways as well. When a sheep or goat wandered away from the safety of the barn, the children went in search of the missing animal. Searching across the farm, the children took hay and grain to tempt the lost sheep or goat into returning to safety. Sometimes the trick worked and sometimes hay wasn't enough. In her memoirs, Alice describes how she found one of their missing sheep:

> One late spring a sheep disappeared. A month passed and the family was puzzled. One day I was following the goats past a "pit" beyond the south fence. I heard a bleat from a deep pit that was about fifteen feet across. When I looked into the pit, there stood the lost sheep. Brother Dave and [Dad] were able to pull up the sheep with a rope.

The animal was thin and thirsty but had survived by eating leaves and shrubs found in the pit. Although the Murrays allowed their herds to roam free, the lost sheep's misadventure was an exception, not the rule. More often than not the free-range animals remained safe in the open fields of the Depot Slough Valley.

Hugh and Minnie kept their children busy, but they still had time to run, play, and occasionally have an adventure. About 1913, as Alice recalls, the first Model T reached Toledo. The automobile was owned by A.T. Peterson, who ran a livery stable in town. One day while driving his new touring car, Mr. Peterson saw Hugh, Alice, and Lucy entering town in the old wagon. He stopped and offered the girls a ride. With Hugh's permission the girls timidly climbed in and were thrilled to ride up and down Main Street several times.[2]

Automobiles weren't the only new adventure during 1913. The Toledo—Siletz Railroad & Navigation Co. constructed a private logging railroad that passed north through the Murray property.[3] A crew of twenty-five Greek workmen did the actual construction work. Lucy's memoirs describe the crew making its way past the farm:

> I remember when the logging railroad was under construction up the valley, while Dave, Lucy and I sat on a hill safely watching the work progress up the Depot Valley to the vast timber

reserves to the north. We could hear the pile driver machine forming the foundation of bridges across the Depot Slough. Much noise and activity for small girls perched on a hill to watch. Before long a track was laid and the donkey engine chugged along, nearer and nearer. Finally the track progressed beyond our sight and hearing. The smoke and whistles thrilled us.

The railroad was used to supply logs to the Toledo Lumber Company. The logs were railed to a dumpsite alongside Depot Slough near Toledo where they were dumped at high tide and then floated to the mill.

For years the children enjoyed spending their free summer hours in the warm water of Depot Slough. The incoming tide backed up at least two feet of water, as Alice records:

> The ocean's tide ran regularly on past our place [on] Depot Slough. When the tide was "in" the streambed overflowed the banks at times. This water would be pleasantly warm for swimming from June through September.
>
> We learned to swim in the Depot Slough, which ran through our tideland. We used water wings as we learned to swim.[4] Friends often joined

us. I helped non-swimmers to gain confidence and skill by holding tightly to whatever garments the friend was wearing. Usually overalls with suspenders to grip across their shoulders.

Living next to Depot Slough provided the Murray children with other adventures besides swimming, namely fishing along its banks. Using worms, a hook, and a string tied on a willow pole, the children easily caught their dinner. Adolescent salmon, or *shiners* as the children called them, made fine meals. During an outgoing tide the children would wade into the shallow water with its sandy bottom and delight in stirring up baby flounder living there while they matured.

While the children were growing up, dairying was becoming an ever more important source of income for Lincoln County farmers.[5] By 1911, practically every farmer had from five to a dozen milk cows.[6] The Murray's owned five.

Dairying in Lincoln County dated back to the opening of reservation lands in 1866 when the first farm settlers arrived bringing their family cows. Excess milk and butter were sold or bartered with neighbors. In 1895, a group of local farmers united to

200

start a dairy processing co-op in Toledo.[7] This first co-op lasted only a short time. In 1899, a second attempt to establish a dairy co-op also failed.[8] Meanwhile, farmers sold their excess cream to a creamery collection station in Toledo, and the product was sent to a processing plant in Corvallis. Some farmers began to deliver raw milk to homes in Toledo.[9]

In 1911, *Sunset Magazine* published an informational booklet called "Toledo, Oregon."[10] The booklet discusses the potential of the dairy industry in Lincoln County:

> The common grade cow nets its owner from $65.00 to $80.00 per annum. Where better milk producers such as Jerseys are kept, the profits run to $100.00 and more per cow.

The article provided the spark that the Toledo area farmers needed to successfully organize themselves.

49. *The Southern Pacific Railroad promoted the settlement of the Pacific Coast through* Sunset *Magazine, 1911.*

The following year, with the incentive of a weekly cash income encouraging them, the farmers finally established a successful dairy co-op where they could manufacture butter and ice cream.[11] In 1913, the Toledo Cooperative Creamery Association was organized, and Hugh Murray was a founding member. According to Port of Toledo meeting notes from April 30, 1913, the association leased waterfront property from the port for $5 a month, and members built a small processing building on the site.

50. Toledo Cooperative Creamery Association, 1913-1927, is pictured in 1918. It was named the Toledo Creamery from 1927 to 1958.

THE TOLEDO CREAMERY

IS OWNED BY LINCOLN COUNTY FARMERS

"Patronize Home Industry"

51. Toledo Cooperative Creamery Association advertisement, 1923.

Although interested in the financial reward his cows could produce, Hugh had little tolerance for milking. He was reared like most farmers of the nineteenth century to believe that milking and butter making were "women's work". When he sat down to do the milking he was often annoyed, sometimes hitting the cows. His impatience made the animals nervous, resulting in less milk production. Alice, recalling her father's behavior, later writes, "Far better for a quiet woman to milk." So . . . Minnie did the milking.

Minnie, and eventually her daughters, milked their five cows twice a day, netting about thirty-plus gallons per day. The warm milk was immediately set aside to allow the cream to rise. Most of the cream was taken to the co-op for processing.

Cream set aside for home use was divided, part used for baking and part turned into butter. Minnie used a five-gallon churn with a lid and long-handled plunger, called a dasher, to make her butter. The churn was often set in a large pan of warm water to shorten the churning time. As she worked the dasher, the churned milk thickened until small balls of butter formed. The balls were patted together and rinsed with several clear cold-water baths, resulting in a nice, even butter pat. Minnie used salt to preserve most of the home butter for winter consumption. Everyone liked the salted butter except for Hugh, who preferred his butter unsalted.

When Alice grew big enough to work the dasher, Minnie taught her how to use the churn. Alice kept a large spoon close by to scrape the cream back into the churn when it escaped out around the dasher. She enjoyed eating the delicious scoops as the warm cream worked its way out around the dasher's handle. The treat was an anticipated benefit when Alice helped her busy mother.

Alice's help freed Minnie to work on other chores. Besides doing the milking Minnie also kept the family clothing in order, spending hours sewing by hand. Lucy describes in her memoirs how that changed the day two traveling salesmen surprised Minnie with a gift:

> In 1914, two Singer Sewing Machine salesmen, Keiffer and Galliane, often stopped overnight at our home on their way to Siletz to sell machines, so one day they gave Mom an old machine, (not Singer), taken in on trade when they sold a new Singer, to pay for all the meals and accommodations she had provided. What a happy day that was. Now mending and new sewing could be done in a fraction of the time it took to be done by hand. The only name that could be found was the word "Faultless" in gold letters on the arm. [Mom] thought perhaps it was put out by Montgomery Ward & Co. It was used steadily until about 1949.

With the ease and speed of the sewing machine, forty-six-year-old Minnie found some relief from the time-consuming hand sewing so much a part of her days. She soon became as adept at machine stitching as she had been with her hand needle.

In 1913, Hugh purchased a sturdy utility horse he named Babe. Used for hauling, clearing, and planting, Babe was also essential for delivering produce to Toledo and Newport. The horse served the family for over twenty years.

While the children were small, Hugh and Minnie educated them at home. By 1915, David and Alice had passed the age when their friends had started classes. Hugh and Minnie decided it was time to enroll the children in the nearby one-room Stanton School.[13] This school, like most one-room schoolhouses of the day, included students from grades one through eight who met and studied together.

In May 1915, Minnie took seven-year-old Alice and eight-year-old David to visit the school to make enrollment preparations for the following school year. Stanton School was located on a ridge near the neighboring Olalla Slough Valley. As the three of them walked, they followed an established trail heading east over the ridge between the two valleys. The mile-and-a-half journey included short steep grades, flat areas, and a small hill. The trail challenged the stamina of its youngest walkers.

The Murrays' first visit to the school intimidated Alice. When they arrived she was shy and refused to play with her girlfriends who were already attending class, choosing instead to cling to the veranda post in front of the school building. David didn't share her misgivings. He was older, bolder, and more confident.

52. *Winter at Stanton School during the first school year for Alice and David, 1916. The arrows point to the Murray children and their teacher, Borgny Romtvedt.*

A month after enrolling in school, David received a small rifle for his ninth birthday. Ever since the Murrays had moved to the farm, they had faced the ongoing problem of wild animals destroying crops. Hugh sternly coached David about gun safety and then put him in charge of protecting the farm.

When orchard cherries were ripe and vulnerable to hungry birds, David sat under one of the three cherry trees and shot robins and any other birds as they came to eat the fruit. Some days the children skinned the birds and cooked the tiny breasts as a treat. David was never cruel or irresponsible with his rifle, even at a young age. He protected the crops and enjoyed being outside.

As summer gave way to fall, David and Alice prepared to start school.

14
Notes

1. Wallis Nash, *Oregon: There and Back in 1877* (Corvallis: Oregon State University Press, 1977), 203.
2. A few years later the livery stable evolved into Peterson's Garage and prospered for many years.
3. Lloyd Palmer, *Steam Towards the Sunset: The Railroads of Lincoln County* (Newport, OR: Lincoln County Historical Society, 1982), 90.
4. Rudy Thompson, in a telephone interview by the author on August 8, 2007, described the water wings he used in the 1920s: "When we were just learning to swim, I had a pair of water wings. They were made of tightly woven cloth. Like real lightweight canvas. When the cloth got wet, you blew it up, and tied the tube."
5. Ralph Selitzer, *The Dairy Industry in America* (New York: Books for Industry, 1976), 323. In 1920 several million dairy farmers around the United States owned herds of twelve or fewer cows. These farmers supplied dairy products to their local areas.
6. Toledo, Oregon, Development League, "Toledo, Oregon" (Portland: *Sunset Magazine* Homeseekers' Bureau brochure, July 15, 1911).
7. Selitzer, 323. By the turn of the twentieth century, seventy percent of farmer

cooperatives in the United States were dairy associations.

8. The second attempt resulted in a local dairy processing plant owned by J.F. Stewart and Sam Center.

9. The first pasteurized milk for sale in the Toledo area was available in 1925.

10. Toledo, Oregon, Development League, "Toledo, Oregon" (brochure, September 1, 1911). *Sunset Magazine* began publishing in 1898 as a promotional magazine for the Southern Pacific Railroad. The magazine was designed to counter the negative "Wild West" image people on the East Coast had of the West Coast. Several brochures on Toledo were published: "The mission of this folder is to interest the homeseeker—to get him to investigate conditions, in the belief that what we have to offer will appeal to him."

11. *Lincoln County Leader*, May 24, 1924.

12. Stanton School was built on the west ridge of Olalla Slough and should not be confused with the Stanton School located in Toledo at that time.

15
Learning Life's Lessons—The Murray Children in and out of School

On the morning of September 13, 1915, David and Alice were eager to attend their first day of school. By pre-arrangement with Minnie, their teacher, Borgny Romtvedt, had placed both children in the first grade so she could assess their skills before advancing them.

To be sure everything went well, Minnie walked over the trail with the children to school. When they arrived they discovered they'd forgotten something. Neither Alice nor David had the required notebooks or writing materials. David was calm, but an embarrassed Alice began to cry. Miss Romtvedt quickly sent the children home so they could buy the proper supplies that day.

When they reached the farm the children told their uncle Simon, who was visiting, what had happened. Simon volunteered to ride his horse to town to get the necessary supplies. The children were delighted. The next day they returned to school with everything they needed and quickly found a place for themselves among their classmates.

The children were enthusiastic students, rarely missing class, even in bad weather. One winter morning as the wind tossed the trees about, the young Murrays sloshed through the rain. Alice and David reached the school to learn they were the only students to attend that day.

In the one-room school, Alice listened attentively as the older students recited poems. She decided to memorize them on her own. Longfellow's "The Village Blacksmith" was the first one. The poem's flowing rhythm, alternating rhyme scheme, and vivid imagery helped make the verse easy for her to remember.[1] Although David wasn't drawn to memorize poems, he also showed interest in his studies. The children's efforts paid off. The following school year, Alice and David skipped the second grade and were promoted to the third grade. Having already memorized the third-grade poems, Alice was ready to recite them in class.

53. *Alice Murray's report card, Stanton School, 1916.*

David had also kept up with his schoolwork, but spent his spare time working with his hands. Like most boys his age, David carried a pocketknife. Those were the days when a pocketknife was a boy's best friend. David's classmates often called on him to sharpen their pencils. He used his knife to cut string for fishing line and a slender willow for the fishing pole. In the springtime, David carved wooden chains from green alder and made whistles when the sap started to flow in the willows.

At home Minnie and Hugh encouraged their children to join in family conversations during meals. The children often shared events from their school day. As Lucy listened to her older siblings, she knew she was missing something by staying home. She pestered her parents to let her start school the following school year. Lucy was six and a half years old in the fall of 1916. Minnie and Hugh had reservations about letting Lucy start school at that age, but she won the argument and started class with her siblings.

Alice writes that the mile-and-a-half long walk to school was quite a challenge for Lucy, especially going up the steep side of the ridge:

> On our way to school, David and I constantly found little Lucy lagging behind as we walked rapidly up the steep grades. We took her hand and almost pulled her along offering encouragement.

Once at school, though, Lucy applied herself with the same diligence as her older brother and sister. She learned quickly, and the school year flew by.

As fall turned to winter and the 1916 holiday season approached, the students drew names for gift giving. They could give anything they wished as a present. There was only one rule: no present should cost more than ten cents. Alice loved her gift—a coloring book with watercolor paints.[2] This was her first store-bought coloring book. To keep the pages neat she painted the pictures carefully, making sure to keep the book from becoming rumpled. The Christmas gift was a highlight of Alice's school year, and she saved the book for many years.

In her memoirs Alice relates that while Lucy proved herself a good student, her age still posed a problem for her mother:

> Lucy excelled and finished the first two grades during that first year. Our mother spoke to the teacher who would be teaching Lucy in the 3rd grade, suggesting that Lucy was so young she should not be promoted beyond one grade per year.

The teacher listened to Minnie's concerns and kept Lucy with similarly aged classmates. Although Lucy may have been disappointed, she had all summer to accept her mother's decision.

The summer of 1917 was like many summers on the Murray farm. The children spent their vacation days outside in the sun, performing chores and tending the family herds on vacant land not far from home. Since the children were away from home most of the day, they took their noonday meal with them. Alice's favorite packed lunch included white navy beans seasoned with sharp cider vinegar. She ate the tangy beans cold as she sat in the warm pasture grass or cool shade of a tree.

One day Peter Henningson, one of the Murray neighbors, came to the farm to help Hugh with a project. By late afternoon the work wasn't finished, so David and Alice, along with a visiting friend, were sent to the Henningson farm to feed the hens before they went to roost for the night. Years later Alice recounts the trip:

> It was nearing evening as we hurried along the road. Little Lucy remained at home. She, being too small and slow to make the speedy trip before dark. I will never forget that evening, though it

seems almost a dream now. We had never seen or heard a live bear before. But we knew from pictures to clearly recognize them on sight. Not too far down in the hollow we heard these frightening woofs and noises. Bears we thought. On our return we passed the same place with fearsome thoughts. Again the strange animal "voices." I saw two bears running and scrambling over a large fallen log, running away from us. We flew by and on home, mainly downhill, as fast as our bare feet could carry us. "Bears, bears," we panted the story to our parents. Father scoffed and told us we had seen some black cattle. "Oh no, I saw two bears and we heard them too," I insisted.

Now these recent years when television shows bears "woofing" and "talking" on the screen, it still reminds me of those wild bears some seventy years earlier. The identical vocal sounds, half growling, half woofing.

That summer Hugh found yet another way to augment the family income. He took Alice and Lucy to a farm auction where he bought a hand-turned cider press for $15. Ten-year-old Alice and seven-year-old Lucy became responsible for gathering all the ripe apples that fell in great numbers throughout the orchard. The girls washed and prepared the fruit, trimming off any

219

bird damage or spoiled portions as they went. When they had several baskets ready to process, they met their father at the press. As the girls placed apples in the crusher, Hugh turned the grinding gear, crushing the apples before pressing the mass into sweet cider. They sold the refreshing cider for twenty-five cents a gallon. When Alice grew strong enough to turn the press wheel, Hugh passed the job on to her. Alice and Lucy made many gallons of apple cider for their dad to sell on market days.

The children spent clear summer nights outside with their mother, learning about the constellations overhead as the stars moved slowly through the skies. Evenings inside the house continued to be family time. As Alice remembers in her memoirs, everyone took turns reading aloud in front of the fire:

> Grandfather subscribed to the Socialist paper "Appeal to Reason" with cartoons of rich plutocrats and Eugene V. Debs the Socialist. Another paper which the whole family loved and read was the Canadian paper, "The Family Herald and Weekly Star" from Montreal. In later years, Grandfather subscribed to the "Spokesman Review" of Spokane, Washington. . . read by all the family.

We also subscribed to several farm papers from which we read aloud the continued stories.

The wide variety of magazines the family read shows that although Minnie, Hugh, and Grandfather David were living a conventional farm life, their philosophies hadn't strayed too far from the ideology of Berlin Heights and Liberal. Everyone enjoyed reading the many perspectives featured in the various periodicals and the conversations those viewpoints sparked.

Although World War I had a direct and powerful impact on Lincoln County, neither Alice nor Lucy writes much about the war's impact on their lives. During the war ten-year-old Alice became interested in reading the world headlines as the family kept abreast of international events and was awed by the activities of hundreds of soldiers working in the area. But the girls were still children and more interested in events that affected their day-to-day lives at home. The thousands of soldiers stationed throughout Lincoln County didn't seem to affect them.

15
Notes

1. Nancy Green Petterson, in an interview by the author on August 15, 2008, recalled that when she and her mother Alice made a trip to the East Coast in 1985, they visited Concord, Massachusetts. While there Alice recited "Concord Hymn" by Ralph Waldo Emerson to Nancy. "She recited the entire first half of the poem about Concord, then she says, 'Oh, I'm so stupid, I can't remember the rest of it.' Well, didn't she have it for what, seventy years? So after we got home she remembered the other half, wrote it out and sent it to me."

2. Brown wrapping paper recycled from store-bought purchases was the children's usual drawing and play writing paper. At that time store purchases came wrapped in brown paper tied with a string.

16

"After sixty years I can still thrill to the joy of those garments."

The summer of 1917 gave way to fall and the new school year began. Lucy entered the second grade. Alice and David were promoted from the third to the fifth grade, finally catching up with other classmates their age.

That fall Minnie became quite ill. While she was sick David stayed home from school for several weeks to help his grandfather with the family chores. This included milking the cows twice a day, tending the garden, and helping Hugh care for Minnie. The girls helped with chores after school. Although Lucy and Alice say very little in their memoirs about David's reaction to missing school, his weeks away didn't hurt his studies. He quickly caught up once back in class.

Ethel L. McLellan was Stanton School's teacher for 1917. She was an innovative educator and believed her students would benefit from a warm noonday meal. She organized a simple hot soup program popular with the children. The students worked in teams as they made their lunch together. One or two students volunteered to bring a quart of milk, another furnished potatoes, another onions, etc. The ingredients were put together in a pot and cooked on the school's wood-burning heater/stove. The hot soup program had the dual benefit of being healthful and teaching teamwork. The meals also introduced the students to new tastes.

Most days the soup would be something familiar. One day, however, the soup had an unexpected ingredient: oysters. The soft bodies made a lasting and not precisely positive impression on Alice:

> I had never eaten oyster soup. I was not too happy with its flavor. But I ate my bowlful and said nothing. The dark stomach portion as well as a bit of sand or gravel added to my dislike.

Alice also tried a barley soup she preferred to forget:

A barley soup was not too tasty but everyone ate his or her portion. Children ate what was offered those days, keeping their opinions to themselves.

Alice may not have cared for some of the results, but she enjoyed taking part in the process:

I was proud to bring a quart of canned corn on two occasions. No one else offered to bring home canned corn because no one raised much corn if any, and none canned any.

Once I volunteered to make the potato soup, though only ten years of age. I trotted up and down the aisle to stir and check the kettle's contents, quite proud of myself.

All in all, Alice preferred her mother's cooking:

A few times during springtime when hens were laying well, the older girls prepared custard. Each brought eggs and milk. These girls used cornstarch. I secretly thought the custard my mother made at home was superior, with no cornstarch. But with the top of the stove preparation, no doubt the cornstarch was necessary for firm custard.

Delicious was the verdict from the class.

Miss McLellan's creative lunch program focused on a positive learning environment.

54. Ethel Lillian McLellan, Stanton School teacher, September 10, 1917-May 24, 1918.

During the same school year, Alice sold magazine subscriptions to earn a premium:

> When I was 10 years old I sold two or three subscriptions to a "Comfort" magazine. I had tried to earn a pretty bracelet, but lacked the number of subscriptions to earn that premium. I settled happily for a sparkly ring.
>
> Hoping to call attention to my new ring, I walked up the aisle in school patting my hair or fussing with my ribbon bow. Some pupils noticed all right. A murmur spread among the 25 to 30 pupils in the room. Both boys and girls noticed which gratified me. Miss McLellan, our teacher who was adored by all of us, was 24 years old and engaged to be married. She added to the admiration and excitement by taking my hand, holding it aloft, while calling the attentions of all to the new shiny ring and stone set, plus admiring it herself. So this memory lingers on forever. This ring was worn for a year or so and then disappeared. I was saddened to lose it.

Miss McLellan's thoughtful comments added to Alice's pleasure and reinforced her willingness to work for what she wanted.

With her talent for sewing, Minnie made all of Lucy's and Alice's dresses. The girls could show her a picture of any dress style they admired and watch their mother create a similar dress. Minnie's design skills allowed her to create a pattern for any outfit she saw, whether in a picture or on someone. At the start of each school year, Minnie made the children new sweaters, raincoats, and other clothing. Toward spring Minnie brightened their lives enormously when she made more new garments for each of the children.

During cold winter weather, most schoolgirls wore long underwear made of cotton, except for one or two girls at school who were referred to as "city types." The long underwear kept the girls warm, but the ends could be seen bulging underneath their black cotton stockings. As the weather warmed, Alice and Lucy either rolled the ends of this underwear neatly above the knee or left the long underwear off completely.

When black sateen bloomers with elastic at the waist and above the knee came into fashion, the girls were smitten with the shiny fabric. They liked the stylish clothing and were proud to own a pair of the fashionable bloomers. In 1977, Alice wrote of her childhood excitement: "After sixty years I can still thrill to the joy of those garments."

Although the girls took great pride in their mother's talent, for Alice and Lucy not even Minnie's skillful sewing could negate the allure of store-bought dresses. After World War I, lightweight chambray dresses sold for $2.98 to $4.98 as advertised in a mail-order catalogue. The dresses were pretty, but Hugh and Minnie had very little cash available. When these dresses were again offered the following year as a collection for $1.98, Minnie bought two dresses apiece for Alice and Lucy. The girls were overjoyed to have store-bought dresses for the first time and wore them proudly.

As the century's second decade neared an end, the Murrays spent the long, wet winter months in a comfortable routine of chores, games, and neighborhood visits. Their evenings included quiet gatherings around the stove where they could relax from busy days, read stories, and sing songs. On summer nights, the children watched the constellations as they passed across the sky. The three children were excelling in school and the farm was a success. Everything seemed secure and predictable. Then a letter from Hugh's sister Adaline altered the everyday life of the close-knit family.

17
Grandfather David's Legacy

Lydia Ann Sellers Murray, matriarch of the Murray family, died in 1918 at age eighty-three. She was buried in Nebraska where she had been living with her daughter Adaline since 1909. Her passing had a profound impact on the Murray family over twelve hundred miles away. Within months of Lydia's funeral, Adaline arrived in Toledo to take her eighty-year-old father back to Nebraska. Neither Alice nor Lucy explains why Adaline came for their grandfather or why he left. All Alice writes is that Adaline came for her grandfather.

55. Adaline Murray Nelson with her mother, Lydia Ann Sellers Murray, her son, Dale, and her husband, Tony Nelson, 1909.

After living in Oregon for nine years, Grandfather David had become an important part of the family. He was the ideal farm hand, so Hugh enjoyed talking and working with his father. Minnie was thankful for his generosity and familial support. The children adored him. The whole family promised to keep in contact through letters, and their correspondence started immediately. There was much to tell Grandfather David. One of their first letters told him about a used upright organ Hugh bought from a retired schoolteacher. Almost twenty years old, the organ was still in admirable condition. The $45 purchase price included a fine variety of music books.

Eleven-year-old Alice immediately started learning to read and play the music. She enjoyed practicing simple, familiar hymns and other tunes as her fingers moved across the keyboard. Eight-year-old Lucy also enjoyed learning to play. So did Minnie. Hugh often joined in playing duets with his fiddle or singing along. The organ provided many hours of pleasure for the family.

Although the Murrays didn't make overnight trips away from the farm, an exception was made in the fall of 1919. Minnie, Alice, and Lucy enjoyed a holiday on the coast while Hugh and David stayed home. Alice's description in her memoirs shows the strong bond mother and daughters shared:

In September 1919, Father took Mom, Lucy and I to Newport in early September for a week to ten days for a well-earned vacation. Mother loved the ocean but very rarely felt she could leave the home place out the Siletz road. Father drove a horse and small wagon to Newport. We rented a cabin over looking the ocean near Jump-off-Joe, a large rock formation. We brought our vegetables, fruits, butter, etc., buying as few foods as really necessary. We left brother Dave [home] to milk the cows and do what was important. School was not starting till later in September.

We three just loved our carefree days. Roaming the beaches. Mother had a long pole with a hook with which to bring out the fine crabs from tide-pools at low tide. We also had large nails for digging out delicious rock oysters from rocks exposed at low tide. We roamed the huckleberries near by. September is the main month for harvesting these tasty blue berries that spread over acres of land.

While browsing in a bookstore on a rainy day our family had noticed a book by Gene Stratten-Porter, *Michael O'Halleron,* which a teacher at school

234

had read to her appreciative pupils a year previously. Priced at 75 cents, we had no spare cash for books. But we asked the storekeeper if he would be interested in buying huckleberries from us. Yes, he would. So we picked a two-quart honey pail of berries. [We] sat and cleaned them well from small stems, leaves and dried up berries. The storekeeper was pleased and gave 35 cents for the berries. He offered to buy some more. So we picked a second pail full. Mother paid the final five cents, and we had a beloved new book.

It was time for father to come for us or we probably would have picked more berries to sell.

Soon after their vacation ended, the children returned to Stanton School. That November, when the school held its annual Thanksgiving program for the parents, the weather was particularly bad. Determined not to miss any of her children's activities, Minnie walked alone through wind and rain to watch her children perform. She was surprised to see that she was the only parent to attend the performance.

At another winter program that same year, poor weather again kept parents away. This time Minnie wasn't alone as she walked to school. A new family, familiar with cold weather, had recently moved to the Depot

Slough Valley from Iowa. Minnie and her new neighbor, Lizzie Erickson, were the only parents to attend the winter performance.

56. *Lizzie Erickson with her three children, Elroy, Lawrence, and Mary Ellen, in Iowa just before moving to Oregon, 1918.*

Walking to and from school provided David, Alice, and Lucy the opportunity to socialize with their friends and tease new students. When neighbor Rudy Thompson started the first grade at Stanton School in 1919, he walked the trail with the rest of his neighboring classmates. Writing to the author in 2007, Rudy recalled that as the children passed through Bear Hollow the older children, having had a scare of their own two years earlier, teased him:

> One of my earliest memories of life in this community was about starting school. This involved hiking about a mile and a half or more through Bear Hollow, which bordered our property. .
>
> Children came to this school from all directions. Some of the family names that I remember were Wessel, Pond, Hacket, Erickson, and of course the Murray family who lived a short ways down the road from our farm.
>
> At the end of the school day as the children left for home and hiked along the trail, there was a game to play. Someone would run ahead and into the brush and make growl noises like a bear. The Murray and Erickson kids would yell out, "bear" and then everyone would run. I think that I knew it was not really a bear, but I still ran to try to keep up with the big kids.

They headed along the part of the old Siletz road toward their homes, and I went alone through Bear Hollow to my home.

The children's teasing gave Rudy nightmares. His mother, alarmed by his fearful dreams, took him out of school for the remainder of the school year.

Rudy shared another bear encounter the Murray children had that summer, this time a more close-up experience. Herb and Lee Kyniston, two bachelor brothers, lived near the Murray farm. They killed a mother bear when she put her head out of her den in the hollow of an old spruce tree near their property. The bear had been nursing her two cubs. The brothers rescued the cubs and asked Hugh and Minnie if they would bottle feed them for a few days since the brothers didn't own a cow. Hugh and Minnie agreed.

57. Six-year-old Rudy Thompson near the Murray farm, 1918.

The young bears slept in a box placed in the kitchen. Alice recalls the trouble two playful cubs can cause when kept inside:

> The cubs accepted a bottle of milk greedily. . . They were cute as could be and smart. They played and slept. But sometimes they stood up and with their claws...stripped a long tear in the wallpaper. All in play, but a disaster to a poor family who papered a room rarely. After a few of these wallpaper tearings, the cubs were scolded and slapped.
>
> When their owner came for them, he was a welcome sight for the lovable and cute cubs. He kept them for some time. His walls were bare boards. A single man's plain home. Finally the cubs outgrew their welcome. They were sold or given away. It's a great pity they weren't released far from civilization.

At the time the bear-sitting story took place, Depot Slough neighbors were looking for further ways to control their natural environment. For years farmers had considered how best to prevent saltwater from reaching their tideland property. Reclaiming the flood plain would open new land in the lower valley for planting crops, growing gardens, and grazing livestock.

240

The flood plain affected twenty-six families who owned a combined total of 400 acres of tidal property. In 1919, these concerned families formed a committee and petitioned the Port of Toledo for a dike to be constructed on Depot Slough near the edge of town. The Port of Toledo approved the construction of the dike and organized the Lincoln County Drainage District #1 in February 1920. The port planned construction to start later that year.

58. Eleven-year-old Lucy Murray is on the left and fourteen-year-old Alice Murray on the right, 1921. The picture was taken just after the girls returned from swimming in the Depot Slough.

*   *   *

At Stanton School, fair weather meant an increase in outdoor activities. Each spring when the trilliums were in bloom, students went on a class outing to a nearby deserted cemetery. Lucy describes the almost forgotten graveyard:

> Our current teacher would take the entire school up through brush and trees to an old cemetery, with some huge headstones, some erect, some fallen down, some buried by falling and rotting logs and trees. I remember one reading either "Captain" or "Colonel Stanton." I forgot his given name or initials, but assumed the school had been named for him.

The graves were about sixty years old in 1920 and located near the old Toledo—Siletz military road. The neglected graveyard was a reminder of earlier days when the area lay within reservation territory, watched over by Indian agents and guarded by soldiers. Sixty years had nearly erased any sign of the men who had managed the reservation. Crumbling headstones and long-forgotten names marked the passing years.

School field trips weren't the only sign of spring. Each May, Stanton School students and their parents gathered to celebrate the close of the school year. Most parents managed to attend, arriving by horse and wagon or on foot, bringing an abundance of food. There were assorted pies, fried chicken, ham, baked beans, sweet and dill pickles, salads, sandwiches, strawberry shortcake, lemonade, and coffee. Everyone looked forward to the end-of-the-school-year picnic. The meal was delicious, the atmosphere festive, and the picnic popular. The celebration marked the beginning of summer.

When the school year ended, David, Alice, and Lucy had returned to their summer chores and tending herds when they received word from Adaline that Grandfather David had died suddenly due to a brain hemorrhage. His unexpected passing was devastating to the family. In reminiscing about their grandfather's life, none of the children could remember hearing him swear or make an angry comment. Lucy had never known a time without her gentle grandfather nearby. In a letter written by an admiring niece, Grandfather David is referred to as a "lovely refined man." Many who knew him considered him neat, cheerful, and industrious. He once told Alice a popular phrase of the day: "I am a jack-of-all-trades, but a master of none." In truth, he was more like a Renaissance man.

David Murray had been a wonderful teacher, readily passing his skills on to his grandchildren. A simple example was his ability to repair shoes. When Alice was ten years old, her grandfather taught her the rudimentary techniques, and a year later she had an opportunity to use them.

Alice owned a pair of high tops that buttoned up one side. After months of walking to and from school, her shoes were worn and near the end of their usefulness. Without a second pair of shoes, she had to make do with them. One winter morning Alice sloshed to school through the rain and mud in her worn-out high tops. The stormy weather loosened the soles at the toe. She spent the rest of the day sitting at her desk with wet feet. Thanks to Grandfather David's instruction, Alice knew how to sew the flapping soles together. Each time the soles separated, Alice repaired them, never telling anyone.

With her shoes needing constant attention, Alice knew they would have to be replaced, so she made a plan. Mohair prices had reached ninety cents a pound after World War I and wool prices had also increased. The higher premiums meant more money for the children when they sheared their goats. When a check came in for the previous summer's profits, Alice decided to use her $4 share for new shoes. Unfortunately for the young entrepreneur, she ran into an obstacle.

Hugh had read about a disaster in some faraway region and asked Alice to donate her money to the devastated people. Not wanting to protest or to tell anyone about her tattered shoes, Alice agreed. She reluctantly finished the school year wearing the same worn-out shoes. Years later while reflecting on this episode, Alice believed that had she shown her father her torn shoes he would have permitted her to use her money to replace them.

When the weather cleared and Alice tossed her old shoes away, she saw the last of Stanton School as well. The school board closed the school in May 1920, and that summer it was torn down. Wood from the old structure was used to build two new elementary schools, one on the east side of the ridge separating Depot Slough from Olalla Slough and one on the west side. The school board located the west-side school, named Sweetbrier, on land donated by Willard Graves, a neighbor living north of the Murrays. The second school was situated near the highway to Corvallis. Both locations meant less walking for children living in the area.

18
Growing up Murray

Building on the long-anticipated dike across Depot Slough started in the summer of 1920. Named the Dahl Dam, the dike worked as expected. The tidal influence abated, and the flood lands no longer were influenced by salt water. Farmers in the lower Depot Slough Valley made use of the reclaimed tideland from mid-spring to fall when the area wasn't waterlogged. Native vegetation that cows would not eat was removed and the ground prepared to receive plants such as ryegrass, fescue, orchard grass and lotus major, all of which provided good forage for dairy and beef cattle.[1] The tideland on the Murray property containing rich, fertile soil was now suitable for growing crops six months of the year.

59. Plowing on the tidelands near Toledo, Oregon, 1911.

In mid-March Hugh planted one of his fields in early potatoes, selling them for five cents a pound at the first markets.[2] Potato prices always dropped as the season progressed, so Hugh was careful to plant early. Lucy, Alice, and David helped by cutting seed potatoes into chunks with one or more good "eyes." When all was ready the children followed behind Hugh as he and their horse Babe plowed the row. The children carefully placed the seed potatoes in the ground as they walked, ever mindful of their father's strict guidelines. Hugh insisted the children set the potatoes with

250

"eyes" upward, so the sprouts could easily penetrate the soil. The children left the potatoes uncovered as they worked. As Hugh plowed the next furrow, soil from the new plowing covered the previously planted row. When everything went smoothly, the planting was quick and efficient.

Ted W. Cox

60. Northward or freshwater view from atop the Depot Slough dike at the end of Fifth Street, Toledo, Oregon, 2004.

61. Southward or saltwater view.

Coinciding with work on the new dike, building crews started construction on Sweetbriar School. By the fall of 1920, members of the school district realized that the school wouldn't be ready to open until after the new year. District administrators decided to transport students to Toledo for interim classes.

Owners of the Toledo—Siletz Railroad & Navigation Co. were contracted to carry children into Toledo on a flatcar pulled by a speeder[3] that ran on the same track David,

Alice, and Lucy had watched Greek crews build seven years earlier. Ironically the speeder didn't travel very fast, but the novelty of riding to school in the open air must have been exciting for the children, and occasionally for the operator. Rudy Thompson recalled some of the mischief caused by older schoolboys:

> Down the long trestle closer to Toledo, every once in a while, one of the big kids would pull the pin out of the trailer behind the speeder. The engineer would have to back up to get hooked back up again. The guy that ran the speeder was unhappy. We got cussed out and of course nobody knew who did it.

Although the transportation arrangement worked well for most of the local families, Minnie and Hugh decided David, Alice, and Lucy could wait for classes to begin at Sweetbriar. The children found themselves enjoying an extended holiday. Lucy and Alice quickly made good use of their time.

Lois Canady, whose family owned a small sawmill business in the Willamette Valley, invited thirteen-year-old Alice and ten-year-old Lucy to stay with her for a few weeks. The three girls planned to pick hops during

October. Hugh and Minnie agreed, and the sisters traveled inland.

Each morning one of the Canady brothers drove the girls from the family farm to the hop yards and then came back for them in the afternoon. The arrangement worked well. The girls spent the day chatting as they gathered hops. None of the industrious young women broke any picking records, but the three of them earned a few dollars and had a good time working outside and away from home.

When hop season ended, Alice and Lucy returned to Toledo. They kept busy with their farm chores and individual interests until Sweetbriar opened in January.

The following spring the children helped Hugh prepare the reclaimed tideland for planting. Hugh and Minnie found the floodplain garden an exceptionally fertile and productive plot. Alice writes about the Murrays' first harvest during the summer of 1921:

> From late October to late spring the rains usually flooded these lands. Then for six months these acres were valuable. Mother planted a large garden and sold the surplus produce. Father had a large field plowed, upon which he scattered turnip seed. The moist soil

produced tender sweet turnips, which he sold in bunches to a produce company for markets in cities.

The success of the tideland gardens had made lobbying for the dam by area residents worthwhile.

After Hugh planted oats in the lower field, David's responsibilities to protect the family crops expanded. He still kept birds away from the ripening fruit, but he also guarded the growing oats from pigeons. On those days when a few unlucky birds crossed David's rifle sight, Minnie cooked pigeon and dumplings for dinner.

In the fall of 1921, David and Alice started their last year of formal education and their second year at Sweetbrier School. They graduated from the eighth grade the following May.

After graduation, sixteen-year-old David found a temporary job at Willard Graves' dairy. David, like his uncle Simon, did not intend to spend his life working on a farm. A short time later David started a lifelong career working in the woods.

As a young boy Rudy Thompson spent quite a bit of time visiting the Murrays, and he later talked about David's first logging job:

> When Dave started working in the woods as a whistle punk, he had an important job. He had to relay a message from a choker setter to the out of sight steam donkey operator called a "donkey puncher" by jerking a wire which led to the whistle on the donkey. An incorrect signal could cause injury to someone. . . I think of this because so often from our farm we could hear these whistle signals coming from logging operations to the north of us.

David quickly found a niche for himself in the logging industry. Before long he was spending the majority of his time working among the trees.

While David was away from home, fifteen-year-old Alice wanted to attend high school. She wished to continue her education but met with unrelenting resistance from her father. To Hugh's way of thinking, U.S. schools were a waste of time after the eighth grade. To ensure Alice fell in line with his decision, he applied as much emotional pressure on the teenager as he could. He gave her no choice but to stay at home and work on the farm. The peace-loving Alice conformed to her father's plans.

Recognizing her father's stubbornness, Alice looked for other ways to feed her desire for further learning. She bought some ninth grade textbooks from a neighbor who had dropped out of high school. While studying the curriculum, she found the math too difficult to learn on her own while the history and English texts were repetitions of what she'd already studied. Disappointed, she set the books aside and abandoned her dream.

To compensate for the absence of high school, Alice focused her drive for learning by memorizing poetry and reading borrowed books. Books brought to her the outside world. From that point on, Alice rarely went anywhere without a book in her hand.

Alice's struggle with Hugh over secondary education brought out her father's non-flexible attitude. When his children were little, he appeared to share a warm and loving closeness with them, but during their teenage years the relationship became more adversarial. While this shift can happen in many parents' relationships with their teenagers, Hugh's unbending attitude went beyond keeping Alice from continuing her education.

David knew first hand the lash of his father's intolerance. Hugh believed in corporal punishment for boys. When disciplining his son, he made David select the switch Hugh would use to strike him.

While this was a common parenting technique during those years, sometimes Hugh's discipline went too far. When he was teaching David to play the violin, sometimes Hugh would whack him with the bow if he made a mistake. Hugh would say sarcastically, "Well, you didn't hit that tone right. Are you tone deaf?" Fifty years later David still had scars on his fingers and wrists from those whacks.[4]

Descended from a fierce Highland ancestry, Hugh struggled with his temper throughout his life. He passed this confrontational instinct on to David. By his teenage years, David had learned to fight his way through disagreements. Both Murray men were liked and respected, but their tempers were also legendary. The day finally came when Hugh's unreasonable temper caught up with him.

62. *David Murray playing at Dorothy and Tony Fieber's 50th wedding anniversary on Depot Slough, May 1979.*

By 1922 David was physically bigger than his father. Family friend Charles Burch shared a story told around the neighborhood at that time:

> Old Hugh and son Dave did not get along sometimes. One day they were standing out on the back porch of the house. I'm sure it was in the wintertime or fall. Everybody in those times had a fifty-gallon rain barrel under the eaves. Lots of times you would get low on water and use that rainwater to cook with. That barrel was sitting there full of water.
>
> Dave and the old man got into a hell of an argument. Dave was about twice as big as the old man. He picked Hugh right up and shoved him headfirst into that barrel. Damn near drowned him. If I remember right the old man was unconscious when he pulled him out and laid him on the floor. Old Dave was very hot tempered.[5]

Soon after this incident, David left home.

One day Hugh's temper fell on Minnie while they argued in the front yard. As their conversation deteriorated into a shoving match, Minnie grabbed Hugh's beard while he pulled her hair. The couple fell to the ground and rolled down the hill together.

The encounter upset Minnie tremendously. To protect herself she went to a lawyer in Toledo and took out a restraining order against her husband. The document clearly stated that Hugh wasn't allowed to touch her in any aggressive way. Hugh obeyed the order, and the couple stayed together. When tempers settled, the pair returned to their daily routine and lived in peace.[6]

18
Notes

1. Onno Husing, "Wetland Conservation Plan Inventory" (City of Toledo, Oregon: 1993), 13.
2. Four to five hundred bushels of potatoes could be grown on an acre of reclaimed tideland, according to a 1911 Toledo Development League brochure.
3. Lloyd Palmer, *Steam Towards the Sunset: The Railroads of Lincoln County* (Newport, OR: Lincoln County Historical Society, 1982), 32. The speeder was a motorized track maintenance and crew transport vehicle. In 1918 the U.S. Army built a connecting track from the private log dump on Depot Slough to the Southern Pacific line in Toledo. This connecting line would have allowed the speeder to take the children to Toledo's downtown waterfront.
4. Bill Wilken, telephone interview by the author, May 10, 2007.
5. Charles Burch, interview by the author, written notes, Eddyville, Oregon, January 17, 2004.
6. Wilken, May 10, 2007.

19
"A Lazy Slug"

David had learned to set traps along the streams and hills surrounding the farm. During 1923, eleven-year-old Rudy Thompson spent weekends visiting seventeen-year-old David, who treated Rudy like a younger brother. Rudy recollected following David several times as he checked his trap lines:

> Dave, he ran a trap line around the area. He was catching mink and muskrats, and occasionally a raccoon. One trap line that I walked with him was up in the woods that went clear up to the Siletz River.

David taught Rudy when and how to set his traps, and where the best places were for success. Rudy looked up to David and enjoyed walking through the woods with his hero. He also liked watching David work the hides:

263

> Somehow he burnt out a hollow in a large old stump. Rather than get a barrel or something. He had these hides soaking there in that bark mix. This was in the stump where the tree had been cut down. It was an old growth Doug fir, five or six feet across. I saw this stump and the cavity in the stump.

David showed Rudy how to tan hides just as he'd taught him how to trap. Whenever he'd gathered enough furs, David sold the pelts to businesses outside the Toledo area. His trapping income varied from year to year, depending upon the success of his trap lines.

While David logged and trapped, Lucy focused on her studies. In spring 1923, thirteen-year-old Lucy graduated from Sweetbriar School. Once again Hugh's resistance to formal education caused a problem since he offered Lucy, as he had Alice, no other option than to stay and work on the family farm.[1] Lucy, however, had her own plans. Momentarily blocked from attending high school, she obeyed her father, and waited.

The Murrays saw their share of sadness in 1923. Marion, Ina and Hamilton Sturdevant's grandson, died in Portland. Only thirty-two years old, he left behind his young widow, Margaret, and his daughter, Patricia. On November 8, Lester Starr Jr. died in Corvallis following an operation. Minnie had been close to her older brother, and his loss brought her great sadness.[2]

One intriguing aspect of the Murray family is that so many strong-willed, independent people could live together under one roof. All of them had their own interests and opinions, yet they shared a common sense of family loyalty and duty. During the day they often went in different directions, especially as the children grew older. But they continued to gather for meals, discussing current events, both worldwide and local.

After David left home, Hugh often stayed upstairs in his son's old bedroom where he complained about his health during the cold, dark winter months. Alice writes years later that her father was usually sick during the winter. Lucy, however, describes her dad as "a lazy slug who wanted to stay upstairs and be waited upon." Both daughters agreed that living with their father was never dull. Minnie accepted Hugh's idiosyncrasies and was happy to have him upstairs out of her way.

Over the years Hugh invited a steady stream of out-of-the-ordinary people to spend time and work on the farm. These visitors were clothed, if necessary, and fed and sheltered. Although Hugh could be unbending toward his children, he helped those who sought his assistance, especially if they listened to what he had to say; he enjoyed a good audience. In her memoirs, Lucy depicts some of the characters her father brought home over the years:

> Having only three beds for several years, one for the parents, one for the son, and one for the two girls together, the company had to sleep with Hugh, while Mother slept on the couch, or upstairs in David's bed after he had gone to work in the logging camps.
>
> There was the unfortunate, illiterate, heavy-set Negro man with both feet cut off across the arches in a train accident, so he could scarcely walk. Un-bathed and unlaundered, he became Hugh Murray's bedfellow. Then there was the tall, dark, swarthy Assyrian man with the glittering dark eyes, who helped by carrying water and wood, and who played cards with us two girls, then young ladies, much to our enjoyment. There was the kind, clean, happy, middle-aged Indian, Joe Thomas from Chiloquin, Oregon who helped around the place, washed his own clothes if the women folk didn't insist on doing it for him. He trained for

a Portland, Oregon marathon, hoping he could win some money. He built an Indian sweathouse down in the woods by a clear, cold creek on our place, and dug a deep hole in the creek to plunge into after the steaming sweat in the little igloo-shaped sweathouse. This was an almost everyday ritual with him. Later on, Alice and the oldest Walter Erickson girl, Meredith, tried it out. That was the first and last time. Very likely, the plunge into the icy water clinched their decision.

Then there was the Southern gentleman, a Mr. Davis, clean and pleasant, who claimed he was the great grand nephew of Confederate President Jefferson Davis, and likely was.

At one time, a man with a team of nice horses and a buckboard, with a chicken coop in back with laying hens, and a place for extra hay and/or bedroll, came driving in at Dad's invitation. No doubt this man appealed to Dad because he was barefooted and shabbily clothed, had several weeks' growth of beard over his face, and hair that had not seen a barber for many a moon. . . This man with the team stayed around quite a while. Where else could he get free food and lodging, free hay for his horses, and free chicken feed? . . . After he had been gone for perhaps almost a year, he returned one dark, cold night, tying his horses to his wagon beside the barn, and coming into the haymow to sleep. It so happened that Mom, Alice and I had decided to spend this same night sleeping in the barn. Luckily, Mom was not afraid of man or beast, always calm and optimistic. Alice and I were petrified to hear footsteps tramping past our heads, but Mom gently asked, "Who is it?" When told, she even gave the man one of our blankets, and we were a bit cool as it was. It was so dark no one could see the other, but he went off in a far corner, dug a hole in the hay, wrapped himself in the blanket and everyone weathered it out until morning. Another of Dad's finds was a small, slender, clean, elderly Englishman with all his worldly possessions in a small knapsack. He was a true gentleman, intelligent, very "straight-laced," not given to making jokes or appreciating too many of them from others. He worked hard and long on our farm, which by that time was in quite a state of disrepair, since Mom had no time beyond all the cooking, canning, housework, outdoor chores, preparing the vegetables to sell, making butter and cottage cheese and gathering and washing eggs to sell etc. So this nice Englishman built a new woodshed, with a little room in one corner for Mom's cream separator, and a table for the milk pans to set on for the cream to rise when we did not need or want to use the hand-turned separator. This still left more room for the wood than we ever had before, all nice and dry.

Lucy's narrative illustrates the colorful strangers that came to the Murray place, welcome to stay if they helped with chores and humored Hugh by listening to his never-ending stories. The family's sleeping arrangements varied. Sometimes Hugh moved over and shared his bed with strangers; sometimes he slept alone. Minnie slept in their bed, in the spare bed, on the couch, or in the barn, depending on company or health. The girls slept in their bed or in the barn with their mother. The Murrays adapted.

In 1924, Hugh got word that his sister Sarah Murray Lightbody had died at fifty-eight. She and her husband, James, had spent forty years together and reared six children.

By 1925, eighteen-year-old David was earning good money as a logger. Seventeen-year-old Alice was keeping her mind busy with the variety of books she read, and fifteen-year-old Lucy was biding her time. Both girls tended their herds and helped their parents. Hugh and Minnie were running the farm and making sure the family was safe and healthy. The rhythm of their lives had once again fallen into a comfortable routine. That all changed when Minnie unwittingly placed herself in harm's way.

The Murray goats and sheep roamed freely across the farm. One day while Minnie was working in the yard, she had her back to one of the Angora billy goats nearby. Her movement caught his attention, and he attacked. Charles Burch recalled the incident:

> Mrs. Murray, she was a little tiny woman, very frail. Old man Murray had these old Angora goats. He had a big billy goat with big horns. [One day] the goat knocked [Mrs. Murray] down and damn near killed her. He just pounded her to pieces before someone come along and got it stopped. She was all broken up.[3]

The brutality of the attack shocked everyone. By the time they got the goat away from Minnie she was seriously injured.

63. Angora goats were valued as land clearers as well as for the commercial value of their mohair. Lincoln County promotional pamphlet, 1911.

With only Babe and a farm wagon for transportation, Alice immediately ran to a neighbor asking for help in transporting her mother to the hospital in Toledo three miles away. The family loaded Minnie into the neighbor's car as carefully as possible, but her hip was broken and she was in a great deal of pain. The doctors kept Minnie hospitalized for three months.

The attack affected everyone in the family, and the hospital stay strained the family's finances. The Murrays pulled together, all doing what they could to help. Hugh sold three of their five milk cows to pay the $27-a-week hospital bill. David paid the doctor's charges. Alice and Lucy tended to the farm. Three times a week Alice walked from the farm to the hospital to visit her mother and tell Minnie what was happening at home. The news was both good and bad.

Since the opening of the Toledo dairy co-op in 1913, the Murrays had been consistent cream contributors. The loss of three of their milk cows in 1925 reduced the family's earning potential during a dynamic time in Toledo's dairy history. From 1922 to 1925 Toledo's population tripled from 800 to over 2,500 people. The rapid growth was due to the opening of the huge Pacific Spruce Corporation sawmill. Neither before nor since has Toledo experienced such a spike in population.[4]

With the influx of people came a corresponding increase in the demand for butter and milk. Forced to sell their cows, the Murrays couldn't participate in the dairy boom. But even if they had found the money to replace their cows, they still would have been at a loss. Minnie had been the primary milker.

Once released from the hospital, she had months of recovery ahead. With the help of her family she regained much of her health, but Minnie's fifty-seven-year-old body never fully recovered from the attack. As Charles Burch recalled, "She couldn't hardly whittle around anymore." With her strength and mobility diminished, Minnie could no longer milk five cows twice a day. The family's milk business never recovered.

For such an active woman, Minnie's new limitations must have brought on moments of frustration. Luckily she retained her artistic skills. Confined to the house, Minnie continued challenging herself. In her memoirs, Lucy recounts how her mother took time each day to work on her art, creating fish scale flowers and jewelry:

> Mom made beautiful white and silver hair ornaments of fish scales, fastened on huge hairpins, brooches, etc. The silver leaves were cut from the half-moon shaped pitted silvery part of the huge scale of Tarpon fish caught off the shores of Florida. She had to send there for them. Some were as large as the palm of her hand. On the fish, the scales overlapped, covering this silvery part. She also used smaller scales of

various other fish, purchased closer.
She soaked them, bent them into
centers for roses, and held them with
tiny wires until they dried in that
shape. She dyed the scales many colors
by boiling them in Diamond Dyes. She
would cut and notch the green ones for
leaves, etc. We two girls and Mom got
pretty moss from the Toledo woods to
use on the roses.

Because Minnie didn't confine herself to
just one medium, she kept a supply of glass
beads and fine wire on hand. She often used
rhinestones and smaller beads to fashion
jewelry and sprays for coats and dresses.
None of her jewelry is known to survive, but
both of her daughters write admiringly
about her artistry. Minnie sold her creations
in town where their beauty still found
customers just as they had when she was
younger. The time spent on her art served a
dual purpose—providing an outlet for her
talents and bringing in extra cash.

As Minnie recovered from her accident,
Lucy's patience with her father reached an
end. After two years of waiting, Lucy found
the excuse she needed to break free from
his dominance:

Dad wouldn't dream of letting his
children go to High School, not to those

"Damn Yankee school teachers," who didn't know a fraction of what he could teach them himself at home. I finally got up enough courage to defy him. My best pal in all the world, Audrey Richards, was just starting High School in Toledo. I had waited two years for this incentive. Dad did not speak to me for a month or more, which could not have pleased me more.

Lucy's attitude toward her father wasn't so much rebellion as determination. Lucy respected her parents and remained particularly close to her mother, but she wanted an education. The fact that Hugh didn't push his point harder shows either this respect for his daughter's free will or Minnie's influence. Minnie wasn't prejudiced against a high school education.

Lucy loved attending school and excelled in her classes. Nonetheless, she was on her own when it came to student fees and transportation. Lucy doesn't describe how she made the three-mile trip into Toledo and back during her freshman year. A new school bus route passed by the Murray farm beginning Lucy's sophomore year, making her trip back and forth easier and faster.

While Lucy pursued her education, Alice made her own bid for independence. Although Alice liked to avoid confrontation, she had plenty of backbone. About the time Lucy started high school, Alice decided to bob her hair. The cut was controversial at the time. Actresses like Clara Bow, Colleen Moore, and Louise Brookes made the bobbed look popular through their movies. Young women everywhere accepted the new style. Short hair became synonymous with boldness and rebellion, words that had once been applied to Minnie when she was Alice's age.

Alice liked her neat new hairdo. Hugh, on the other hand, despised the look. He hadn't liked Minnie's short hair when they married, and he didn't like the style of his daughter's hair twenty years later. When Lucy and Audrey Richards bobbed their hair, Hugh complained that the girls had taken a "foolish step." The contented young women ignored his grumbling.

64. Eighteen-year-old Alice, nineteen-year-old David, and sixteen-year-old Lucy Murray, 1926.

As the girls enjoyed their stylish new haircuts, Hugh and David had their own adventure with fashion. Sometime during 1926 they heard that a dead whale had

277

beached in the Newport area, so they decided to gather a quantity of the flesh for rendering.[5] Lucy explores the experience in her writings:

> Sometimes Mom, Alice and I preferred barn sleeping, as after Dad had rendered out rotting whale blubber in a three footed black cast iron pot set down into the wood stove fire, after removing the lid. The whale blubber, which makes excellent shoe grease if one can abide the odor, had been joyfully garnered from a decaying whale, which had inadvertently washed up on the beach at Newport. Of course, this pot had to be full beyond the level of the top. No one who has not smelled burning rotted whale blubber, coursing down the sides of a pot, some into the fire, some out over the stove top, where it formed an impenetrable glaze, could ever conceive what a shambles this could throw an entire house into. Of course, rotting potatoes, overflowing, cooking in this same pot, and burning on the stovetop could run the whale blubber a close second. The whale blubber was a one-time occurrence, except when the grease was warmed each time to put on shoes. It lasted a few years, until it was all gone.

Unlike Hugh, David rendered the whale blubber outside, away from his house. When he finished, he bottled the clarified oil and sold it to loggers who used it to weatherproof their work boots.

David gave a bottle of the scorched grease to fourteen-year-old Rudy Thompson, who used the waterproofing on his school shoes. Looking back at ninety-five, Rudy chuckled when he described the results: "That's when the kids complained that they did not like to sit next to me on the school bus." But peer pressure didn't stop Rudy; he continued using the smelly oil to protect his shoes from wet weather.

While David expanded his entrepreneurial skills, nineteen-year-old Alice and sixteen-year-old Lucy grew into attractive young women and began to date. Dark-headed and beautiful, Lucy had a nice shape, neither skinny nor fat.[6] Alice, described on her driver's license at the time as 5'2" and weighing 108 pounds, had bright blue eyes and was equally charming. The girls were drawn to different types of young men and didn't compete with each other. They were close and remained so throughout their lives.

As the girls interacted with their friends, Alice's quieter personality often let Lucy's vivacity shine in the crowd. Lucy's sociability made her a popular companion, and she dated most weekends. Alice, though more reserved than her adventurous sister, liked to have fun and could be very playful. She spent more time alone with her books than Lucy did, but Alice also had her share of male attention. She dreamed of marrying a tall, dark-haired man who loved literature.

Hugh occasionally encouraged young men to call on his daughters. The girls didn't appreciate this interference, as they preferred to choose their own companions. Most of the time Hugh liked the boys his daughters dated, but occasionally one met with Hugh's displeasure.

Lucy writes that one evening she was entertaining a boy at home, sitting on his knee by the kitchen table, eating cookies and giggling. Suddenly the downstairs bedroom door flew open. There stood old Hugh Murray in his woolen underwear. Looking alarmingly stern with his long hair and beard, he hadn't opened his mouth to reprimand the pair before the young man removed Lucy from his lap, scattering cookie crumbs everywhere. He left abruptly, leaving Lucy on her own to face her annoyed father. By then, Hugh had what he wanted. He grumbled and went back to bed.

As Alice and Lucy reached their late teens, they became more and more involved in activities away from the farm. When a family friend told them about a summer job opportunity, they took it.

19
Notes

1. Nancy Green Petterson, in an interview by the author on August 15, 2008, said Alice had told her that one of the reasons she didn't push harder to go to high school was because Hugh would not have let both girls attend at the same time. Alice knew how much Lucy wanted to go, so she stepped out of the way, giving her sister the opportunity.
2. Obituary for Lester Starr Jr., *Lincoln County Leader,* November 15, 1923.   Lester had spent his last five years working for the Toledo School District. He had also continued to help with the tax rolls for Lincoln County, a job he started in 1893 when the county was first formed. Lester and Hattie had been married for forty-three years, living thirty-three of them in Toledo.
3. Charles Burch, interview by the author, written notes, Eddyville, Oregon, January 17, 2004.
4. *Lincoln County Leader,* August 27, 1925.
5. To nineteenth-century whale hunters, whales were like a swimming oil well. The oil gathered from rendered blubber was used in lubricating machinery, making the Industrial Revolution possible.
6. Bob Green, telephone interview by the author, December 7, 2006.

20
Following the Harvest

The Burch family property lay north of the Murray farm. During the summer of 1927, eleven- year-old Effie Burch, the third of five children, joined a group of migrant farm workers headed for the Willamette Valley. Included in the group were her great-uncle Frank Salisbury and her extended family from Toledo and Agate Beach.

The migrant workers followed various mid-valley harvests between Crabtree, east of Albany, and the Salem area twenty miles to the north. The crews started with strawberries and then picked loganberries, cherries, and pole beans in succession. Throughout the three-month season, a good picker could earn as much as $45 during each three-week harvest. This was a good wage for 1927.

When Effie returned home at summer's end, she enthusiastically told Lucy and Alice about her experience. She encouraged them to join the migrant crew. The following summer they applied for the job and were hired immediately. The summer work was a great opportunity for Alice and Lucy. They had years of experience picking crops, and working in the valley would give them a break from their father.

In 1927, Hugh's brother-in-law James Albert Lightbody died at age sixty-eight in Maine, having spent his last three years as a widower. A few months later the Murrays opened the new year on another sad note. Ina Sturdevant, Minnie's half sister, died at seventy-eight after an extended illness. Ina had been an invalid the last ten years of her life. Like her husband, Hamilton, she had been an active participant in the Toledo community during her healthy retirement years, including membership in the Women's Relief Corps.

In the spring of 1928, twenty-two-year-old David married seventeen-year-old Alice Kyniston. On June 28, the *Lincoln County Leader* announced their wedding:

From Depot Slough

David Murray and Alice Kyniston were married on Monday evening. The bride is the daughter of William Kyniston and the groom is the only son of Mr. and Mrs. H. Murray.

Following the ceremony the couple moved to Mack's Landing, a logging camp near Siletz where David worked as a tree cutter.

As David and his wife settled into their new home, Lucy, Alice, and Effie each bought a $1.50 bus ticket to the Willamette Valley. Their destination was the Betzer strawberry farm near Crabtree.

The girls arrived at the Crabtree bus terminal in the afternoon and expected Burt Salisbury to meet the bus. He wasn't there. They waited but nobody came. Without transportation the girls were stranded with nothing to do except watch their luggage. Come late afternoon, the disappointed farm hands asked the station manager to telephone the Betzer farm. As dusk settled someone finally arrived to pick them up.

Between the migrant field workers and families living near the farm, there were over sixty pickers that season. To house the incoming workers, Mr. Betzer constructed a row of shacks and provided straw for all of his employees to place under their bedding. A covered area outside each of the rooms contained a small wood cook stove. With the warm summer weather these simple accommodations met with everyone's approval.

With people from the Toledo area on the migrant crew, the girls worked with old friends nearby as well as new ones they met while in the valley. The girls were content with their new jobs, although they missed their mother, who had a few plans of her own for the summer.

While Lucy and Alice were in the valley, sixty-year-old Minnie registered for a correspondence course that taught her how to tint photographs in oil. She adapted this technique for tinting Christmas and Easter greeting cards in watercolor. As her skill grew she sold her work to people living in the Toledo area.

Mr. Betzer was a practicing minister and didn't work his fields on Sundays, so his crews worked six days a week with one day off. The pickers often used Sundays to wash their clothes or go swimming in the nearby Santiam River. As the strawberry season came to an end, the girls packed their bags and got ready to leave the Betzer farm. In her memoirs, Alice describes their work on the migrant route:

> After three weeks in the strawberries, we moved on to three weeks of loganberry picking. The loganberry farm was towards Salem at Liberty P.O. This was stand up work, but

loganberries have thorns. At this farm there would be days when the berries were not ripe. There were cherry orchards nearby that needed picking, so it worked out well. I did good at picking cherries. We all enjoyed this change, and we all ate too many cherries. I almost gave myself an attack of diarrhea! Some of the Gray boys did and they lost a day's work.

At one cherry orchard we could hear a man picking. The cherries sounded like a steady stream in his pail as he began on an empty pail. Later the three of us asked the man how he could pick so fast and how many boxes per day he averaged? His total made our picking look mighty small. We picked Royal Annes, Bings, Lamberts and Black Republicans. All large sweet cherries. The stems had to be left attached, as these were fancy for the fresh eating trade. Some of them were shipped as far as New York City. The Royal Annes were generally put into barrels of brine for later processing . . . in the canneries after the rush of fresh fruits were past.

After three weeks of picking logans and cherries we went home for a few weeks until Kentucky Wonder pole beans near Turner and Lebanon were ready near mid-August. All of the pickers including Lucy and I were ready to leave the logans with their thorns and staining of red juice.

We liked the bean picking, no thorns, no berry stains. We were instructed to pick pencil size and up. They were sold to canneries in Salem. We filled a gunnysack, put our numbers on it and left it for the "boys" to carry in and weigh for us. After three weeks in beans most of the coastal crew left for home.

We earned about $45.00 or a little more at each variety we harvested.

Alice and Lucy picked four different crops that summer; at $45 a harvest, the girls earned about $180, equal to about $2,100 today. Since they still lived on the family farm, most of their living expenses were covered. Their summer income gave them the freedom to see a movie, go roller-skating, buy necessities, or splurge on a present for their mother. For Lucy, the money also paid her school expenses.

As the 1928 school year started, Lucy took advantage of every opportunity that came her way. She served as class secretary and editor of "Skookum Wawa," the school paper. The following June, she delivered the valedictory address at graduation. Several years of hard work culminated in Lucy's valedictorian achievement.

65. Lucy Murray, Toledo High School Yearbook, 1929.

After graduation, nineteen-year-old Lucy and twenty-one-year-old Alice again prepared to join the migrant pickers. This time they urged Minnie to join them during the three-week strawberry harvest. Minnie agreed. She knew her body couldn't work at the pace her daughters set, but the three of them hadn't spent any time together away from the farm since their Nye Beach vacation ten years earlier. Lucy and Alice paid Glen Roberts to drive them directly to the Betzer farm.

66. Alice Murray, 1929.

Minnie enjoyed a playful relationship with her daughters. Over the years some of this closeness is shown in the various names Alice and Lucy called their mother: Brindle, Lonnel, and Mason.

When the strawberry season got underway, Alice worked quickly. She soon found herself competing to be the first picker to reach a ton. Her biggest competitor was a young man named Russell Gray. Alice had a competitive streak and relished an occasional challenge:

> The day we reached a ton apiece was hectic. Some dirty work on Russell's part led me to do the same. His parents would carry in the filled crates to the checking stand, offering one of theirs as Russell's. Lucy and I and others saw this. So when one of these crates was checked in as Russell's, I took one of Lucy's as if it were mine, two or three times. He cheated and I cheated. I never paid Lucy back for carrying in her crates to save me. . .

Although she enjoyed the challenge of beating her opponent, Alice didn't dwell on the victory:

> That one day I reached one ton. Russell reached a ton either that day or the

next morning. Then no more sharp competitions. All friends again as the picking ended.

I won the first prize of $10.00 for picking the first ton of berries. Russell Gray was right behind so he was given a second prize of $7.00.

Mr. Betzer gave an ice cream feed to his local and "outside" crews on July 4th. Ice cream and cookies. Nice treat on a hot day.

At sixty-one Minnie had picked well. She may have reflected back to her childhood when she first helped her parents pick strawberries on their farm in Berlin Heights, Ohio. Fatigued but satisfied, Minnie returned home after the three-week season. Hugh was glad to have her back with him. He'd missed reading to her and eating her cooking.

As Minnie left for home, her daughters moved on to the next crop, pole beans on a farm located near Turner. Alice once again found herself with a challenger. This time her competition was a tall sixty-year-old man with lean, broad shoulders and long arms. The two of them were the only ones to pick a ton of beans. The pay for beans was the same as for strawberries: at two-and-a-quarter cents per pound, a ton paid $45. Fast pickers like Alice and Lucy could earn the full amount if they completed the three-week season, which the girls did.

When bean-picking season ended, the girls found themselves with time on their hands. Since Lucy was no longer constrained by school in the fall, they didn't need to rush back to Toledo. Friends on the migrant crew encouraged Alice, Lucy, and two other girls to apply for work in one of the Salem canneries.

The sisters had gained reputations as fast workers and were hired immediately. Their first job was sorting Italian prunes on a moving belt. Then the girls filled the cans with fruit and weighed them; afterward the full cans were transferred along a conveyor belt to be topped with syrup and sealed.

Ted W. Cox

67. Alice Murray wore this cannery employee button on the front of her cap, 1929. [1]

After canning prunes, the girls worked with Kentucky Wonder beans, followed by a long pear season, as Alice explains in her memoirs:

> We enjoyed snipping ends of the beans for so much a box. I liked that and the sorting and weighing cans that followed.
>
> We tried peeling pears @ 27 ½ cents an hour. I was there a day and not speedy. So a floor lady put me to slicing pears, followed by coring and canning. We ended the season coring pears for a month.

Alice and Lucy worked best in the fields where they had experience picking the assorted berries grown by their parents. Working in the cannery was new to them and a change from working out-of-doors. The girls were ready to go home when the canning season ended in October.

But before returning to Toledo, Alice and Lucy splurged on a brief holiday in Salem. They enjoyed the restaurants, took in a movie, and then went shopping downtown. Alice bought herself a $33 Elgin wristwatch that is still in the family. Lucy treated herself to a $10 permanent. After their end-of-season vacation the girls returned home for a quiet winter on the farm. By the end of the year a new Murray had arrived.

Hugh and Minnie celebrated the birth of their first grandchild on December 1, 1929. In keeping with family tradition, David wanted to name his son Hugh after his father, but instead his strong-willed wife named the baby William after her father. David resented the break from family tradition.

68. The Murrays and Ericksons pose for a picture while attending a picnic on the Depot Slough, May 25, 1930. Left to right: Alice Murray, Mary Erickson (Elroy's wife), baby Betty Erickson, and Lucy Murray.

In the summer of 1930, Lucy and Alice returned to their valley migrant jobs. Will Gray, Effie Burch's uncle, had just bought a new Model A Ford sedan and offered to drive

Alice, Lucy, Effie, and Chester Burch to the Betzer farm. After leaving Toledo, the car started up Pioneer Mountain east of town when Will hit gravel on a curve and skidded out of control. The vehicle went over the embankment and rolled twice. Both Will and Chester suffered minor head injuries and were taken to the hospital. Remarkably, none of the girls were injured. Soon the five continued to the Betzer farm, everyone reaching Crabtree safely, though not in Will's car.[2]

Alice and Lucy may not have known at the time, but after three years of following the harvest, the summer of 1930 would be the last time they would work with the migrant crew. The next year, while the United States was beginning to struggle under the grip of the worst financial crisis in its history, a new job opportunity opened for Alice and Lucy closer to home.

20
Notes

1. The Del Monte brand was used originally in 1880s Oakland, California, to supply premium coffee to Hotel Del Monte. In 1892 the business expanded to include canned fruits.
2. Charles Burch, telephone interview by the author, November 27, 2006.

21
The Cooperage and Courting

In April 1928 the world's largest manufacturer of dairy equipment, the Creamery Package Manufacturing Company, opened a butter tub stave sawmill in Toledo. Referred to locally as the Cooperage, the $150,000[1] sawmill was a boon to Toledo's economy, eventually growing into the second largest employer in Lincoln County.[2]

During the spring of 1929 the Cooperage expanded operations, increasing output from 4,000 to 6,000 non-assembled butter tubs per day.[3] After the staves were shipped by railroad to the Midwest, they were assembled into finished butter tubs and sold wholesale to dairy processing plants.

In the winter of 1930, the mill added a new department to cut bottoms and lids for the tubs.[4] Up to that point it had manufactured only the side staves. During this expansion Alice and Lucy were hired to work at the plant. The Cooperage had a unique policy of employing women. Whereas traditionally a sawmill was a man's world, women made up about ten percent of Toledo's butter tub work force. Most Cooperage women worked in the shipping end of the plant and did the final handling of the staves. The female employees were grateful to have work in such hard times and enjoyed working at the mill. Alice and Lucy were hired to sort staves. The girls immediately made friends among their coworkers.

Lucy and Alice were paid twenty-seven cents an hour, and they felt rich.[5] Reared to be thrifty, they saved a good portion of their wages. With $2.16 a day, they had spending money in their pockets and cash set aside in savings. On days when Cooperage machinery broke down, the two weren't paid but enjoyed the time off.

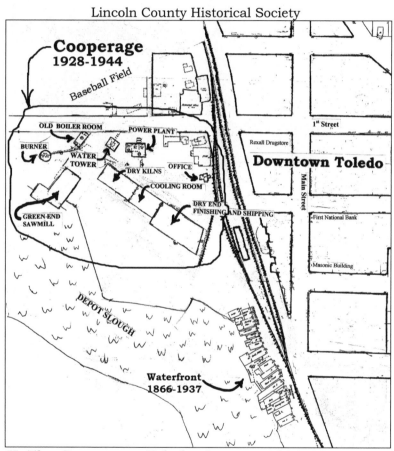

Cooperage
1928-1944

Baseball Field

OLD BOILER ROOM

POWER PLANT

BURNER

WATER
TOWER

DRY KILNS

OFFICE

COOLING ROOM

GREEN-END
SAWMILL

DRY END
FINISHING AND SHIPPING

DEPOT SLOUGH

Waterfront
1866-1937

1st Street

Rexall Drugstore

Downtown Toledo

Main Street

First National Bank

Masonic Building

K. The Cooperage, Toledo, Oregon, 1928-1944.

301

69. Cooperage workers, 1937. Lucy Murray Wade, second from right, has her arm on the shoulder of her future husband, Jim Marrs.

During lunch breaks Cooperage woman enjoyed window-shopping on Main Street. Although women wearing work pants was an unusual sight during the 1930s, the locals admired them.[6]

Charles Burch remembered seeing Alice downtown during these years:

> When I was a little kid we were very poor. My folks didn't have a pot to pee in nor a window to throw it out of. Once in a while we kids would hitchhike into Toledo. There were matinees at the theater. If we happened to be around the Ross Theater when Alice was around, she would buy us tickets. She was working in the Cooperage then. She did the same way over at the skating rink. She used to buy me tickets so I could skate. She was a great gal, always a sweetheart. Lucy was a bit on the wild side.[7]

Work at the Cooperage combined good earnings with a convenient location in Toledo. The three-mile walk from the farm to the Cooperage would have taken Alice and Lucy about an hour each way. Soon the girls saved time by riding to work with other employees.

Lucy and Alice were outnumbered ten to one by their male co-workers. The large dating pool changed their lives. One day while co-worker Roy Green was tending the dry kiln, he noticed twenty-three-year-old Alice sorting staves. He was immediately smitten and quickly found an opportunity to introduce himself. After this initial meeting, Alice and Roy smiled and waved to each other at work.

Ted W. Cox

70. *Charles Burch (photographed in 2007) worked at the Cooperage from 1936 to 1944. He holds a spruce butter tub made in 1937.*

Roy owned a striking 1930 blue Durant coupe with a rumble seat. He drove the car with pride wherever he went:

> One day I was driving home from work and saw Alice walking alongside of the road. I had already seen her working in the Cooperage. I pulled over and offered her a ride. She got in, and from that time on, that was it.[8]

Roy quickly became her "steady."

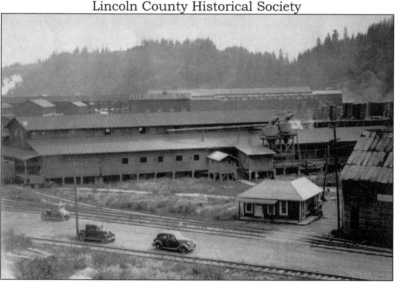

71. The Toledo Cooperage, 1935. Pictured is the building where Lucy and Alice Murray worked. Finished staves were packed and shipped by railroad from the loading dock on the left. The small building housed the company office. The middle car belonged to Roy Green.

Soon after they started dating, Alice invited Roy to meet her parents. Roy vividly remembered meeting Hugh:

> Hugh took a liking to me right away. He had a cheerful smile and good word for all. The day I met him, he showed me around the farm. He pulled a big turnip out of the ground. I said, "Well, Mr. Murray, what do you have there?" He said, "It's a turnip." "Is it good?" "Oh yeah," he replied, and cut me a piece to sample.
>
> Hugh asked if I would like to ride into town. He had a load of fruit and vegetables to sell. I told him that I would like that.

Roy climbed into Hugh's wagon and off they went. From that day forward, Roy and Hugh were good friends. Roy fit nicely into Alice's family.

While Alice and Roy continued to grow closer, David's marriage to Alice Kyniston was disintegrating. The couple had built a home on the lower Murray property in 1930. But having a place of their own hadn't helped them find stability. After three turbulent years their marriage was in trouble.

David, like his father, had a quick temper, a temper he didn't always try to control. One day a serious disagreement with his brother-in-law led to violence. The fight left his young wife shaken. Alice left David while she was carrying their second child, taking two-year-old Bill with her. Because they were unable to reconcile their differences, the separation became permanent. On June 21, 1932, Alice gave birth to Barbara June Murray in Grants Pass, Oregon.[9] David wasn't on hand to meet his daughter.

21
Notes

1. Charles Cooper to his son Milton, 26 March 1928. Excerpted from Cooper family records sent to the author, November 2007.
2. *Lincoln County Leader,* April 6, 1939. By the late 1930s the Cooperage employed over 200 people.
3. *Lincoln County Leader,* February 14, 1929.
4. *Lincoln County Leader,* December 18, 1930.
5. Minnie Murray to Emma Murray, February 21, 1933.
6. Mary E. Dickerson, interview by the author, written notes, Depot Bay, Oregon, August 18, 2003.
7. Charles Burch, interview by the author, written notes, Eddyville, Oregon, January 17, 2004.
8. Roy A. Green, interview by the author, written notes, Philomath, Oregon, July 9, 2003.
9. Bill Wilken, telephone interview by the author, May 26, 2007.

22
Wedding Bells and Babies

In late 1929 the Great Depression began with the collapse of Wall Street and continued until the late 1930s. Many people remember 1931 and 1932 as especially difficult years. This was true for the recently expanded Cooperage sawmill as well. As the mill struggled to keep its doors open, operations were cut back to two-and-a-half days every other week (about five days a month). Basic wages were lowered to twenty-five cents an hour.

Alice and Lucy were not as affected by the lack of steady work as other employees were. Still living on their family's farm, the girls earned enough at the Cooperage to contribute to the running of the household. Their wages bought hay for the cows and grain for the hens, paid the modest property taxes, and purchased what few groceries were necessary. The Murrays weathered the financial storm that was disrupting so many families across the country.

72 .Twenty-one-year-old Lucy Murray, 1931.

73. Twenty-six-year-old Alice Murray, 1933.

In the spring of 1932 Alice and Lucy bought and raised a wiener piglet. The pig grew quickly on milk, cooked cull potatoes, fresh pears, and sweet apples. When the

311

time came to slaughter, the pig had reached 200 pounds. Hugh did the butchering with help from Alice and Lucy. The bacon, ham, and pork chops provided delicious meals.

During the following winter, the Cooperage experienced an upswing in orders. With the mill busy once again, Alice and Lucy started working more hours. They were grateful for the work. In a letter written on February 21, 1933, to her sister-in-law Emma, Minnie described her daughters' busy schedule:

> The girls are still holding down their job. [They] begin work at 7:30 a.m. and quit at 5 p.m. from Monday morning until Saturday, but only work Saturday forenoon, which gives them the chance to do the washings Saturday p.m. and scrub floors, etc. They are pretty busy girls you can imagine, and are lucky to be [in] these hard times.
>
> I probably told you they are doing piecework now, for a number of months and mostly earn a little more than when paid by the hour. At first Lucy beat Alice in the amount of work done, but lately Alice is just about keeping up with Lucy. Some days they earn $3.00 each or a few cents over.

Minnie was proud of her daughters.

In 1933, Louis Powers, a twelve-year-old neighbor, became a regular weekend visitor to the Murray farm. He helped Hugh with chores and often spent the night:

I used to pick on his daughter Alice. I gave her hell. She was out there milking the cow one day and I said, "Oh, it's about time you sat down there on that dead ass and got to milking!" Wow, she shot that old cow milk right up on my face.

She said, "There you are," and laughed. We were always picking on each other.

This one morning, I was so tired. Alice came in and she says, "Louis, it's time for you to get out of bed."

I says, "Yeah, I'll get up pretty soon."

"Now you will," she answered back. She took hold of the covers and pow! She took off with them. Here I laid on the bed, no covers. She had them. She took them out into the other room. I felt, oh God, here a gal pulled my covers off. I got up and came out.

She said, "Well, I knew that you would get up."

I replied, "Yeah, I about froze my rear off."

"That's all right, it didn't bother me," she said laughing.[1]

Sometimes Louis volunteered to do the milking. He told about one afternoon when Lucy came into the barn while he was milking:

> I know how to milk a cow. One time I saw Lucy come in and I took over the teat and *swish*. "Damn you," she says. "I'm going to get you!"
>
> She knocked me off the stool and grabbed the teat and spurt milk all over me. Yeah, Lucy and I had a milk fight. I already drew milk out for the cats. I picked it up and threw it on her. Then she poured milk down my neck. I caught hell for that. Oh man. The old man, he found out about it. When I went to the house, milk all over me, Lucy had milk all over her.
>
> Oh, he gave us hell. "You kids, you are wasting that good milk." He says, "I could have drank that."
>
> Lucy says, "Well, we didn't drink it, you can have it."
>
> Hugh says, "Don't be smart." He was not one to joke around that way.

74. Friends standing in front of Roy Green's 1930 Durant at the Murray farm, 1931. From left to right: Bill Green, Pearl Moe, Lucy Murray, Clarence Moe, Alice Murray, and Roy Green.

As often happens, small and large events moved side by side. While the national economy struggled to rebound in 1933, the bond between Roy and Alice grew stronger:

> I asked Alice to marry and she accepted. I wanted her in the worst way! Ted Cosgrove, the plant manager at the Cooperage, granted my request for a month off for my honeymoon.[2]

After two years of courtship, Alice left the Cooperage to marry Roy Green. Roy was twenty-three and Alice was twenty-six. Roy wasn't the tall, dark-haired, bookish man Alice had fantasized about marrying as a teenager, but he was a talented and hard-working, capable fellow. Alice chose Saturday, July 15, 1933, for their wedding.

To eliminate any strain the wedding might place on Minnie, the ceremony was held at Roy's parents' house in Toledo. Allen and Irene Green welcomed Alice into their family and were happy to open their home for the wedding:

> Roy's home was far from stylishly furnished, but it was decent and satisfactory. Our old home was shabby and poorly furnished.[3]

Like her mother, Alice hadn't grown up with dreams of a big church wedding. A simple ceremony appealed to her:

> A young minister who worked at the Creamery Packaging Company was asked to read the simple words necessary. This was Roy's decision, I had no choice. Even a justice of the peace would have been O.K.

The day before the wedding, Roy went to Thatcher's Barber Shop on Hill Street for a hair cut.[4] During the trim, Roy received some advice he later recounted:

> "Now Roy, I'm an old timer at this and you don't have any experience with this marriage business. So I'm going to tell you what to do on your wedding night."
>
> He got my attention. "O.K., first, get some brand new sheets on your bed. Make it all nice and fluffy. Second, get a see-through negligee for your new wife and have her put it on. Third, when you've done all this preparation, call me."

The haircut was the barber's wedding present to Roy.

While Roy was getting his trim, Alice was getting her hair done by her cousin Margaret across the street at Margaret's Beauty Salon. The next day they married quietly. The July 20, 1933, *Lincoln County Leader* carried the wedding announcement:

> Roy Green Weds Alice Murray on
> Saturday
>
> On Saturday morning at the home of Mr. and Mrs. H.A. Green of Toledo, their son, Roy Allen Green, was united in marriage to Miss Alice Murray, daughter of Mr. and Mrs. Hugh Murray who live on a farm on the Siletz road.

Immediately following the ceremony, the young couple left for a month's honeymoon trip and will visit Yellowstone National Park, also visit relatives in Nebraska. They have the hearty well wishes of the community.

The honeymoon was somewhat curtailed because of a National Bank Holiday ordered in March that year by President Roosevelt. The bank that held their savings remained closed for reorganization and Roy and Alice eventually lost all of their savings.[5] Nonetheless, the couple was happy to leave on their trip. During the honeymoon they stopped in Nebraska to visit with Alice's aunt Adaline and uncle Tony.

When they returned home, the newlyweds settled into a $10-a-month rental house in west Toledo. The house was close enough for Roy to walk to work and return home for lunch. This saved on gas for the car. Alice quickly settled into her role as homemaker:

I began to can corn, beans and beef. We bought a beef shoulder at 25 cents a pound. Any surplus fruit and vegetables grown by our parents was accepted and welcomed. Apples were picked and stored from my parents' extensive variety of apples and pears. Roy drank the canned pear juice. I ate the pears. I canned berries and Roy made cider. We drank the plentiful juice. I often bought fat short ribs to pot-roast. Often eaten with potatoes, carrots and onions. We had two good meals for 35 cents. Roy fished and dug clams to add variety to our meals.

Alice took pride in stretching their resources. Her success ensured the couple ate well as they began their life together.

Ted W. Cox

75. In 1933, Alice and Roy Green moved into their first home at 847 NW Fifth Street, Toledo (photographed in 2003). Owner Eleanor Bogart lived next door. Arriving in 1866, her grandfather was John Graham, the founder of Toledo.

The satisfaction Alice felt maintaining her own home soon increased when she became pregnant with her first child. On the day she delivered, Alice had been very busy. Reflecting back, she felt that her overexertion that day probably triggered the onset of early labor:

> Baby Dolores Lorraine was born May 22, 1934, almost a month before she was due to arrive. . . The pains began 11 p.m. to 12 p.m. By 2 a.m. they were severe enough to justify going for Dr. Burgess. I had not seen Doctors, but Roy had contacted Dr. Burgess, the same Doctor who had delivered me some 28 years earlier. By 7:00 a.m. a seven-pound girl was born. I had no desire for drugs and had no problem after I settled down and made an effort to give birth. The Doctor charged $25.00.

Baby Dolores quickly became known as Dee.

While Alice adapted to her new roles as wife and mother, she didn't neglect her role as Hugh and Minnie's daughter. She often visited her parents to see how they were and to help with chores.

Not long after the safe arrival of Dee, Minnie went on a long overdue holiday. She was encouraged by Alice, who had returned

from her honeymoon with stories of interesting visits and
places. Minnie visited her sister-in-law Adaline in Nebraska and spent some time resting at an artists' commune.

76. Minnie Murray on a visit to Hugh's sister and brother-in-law, Adaline and Tony Nelson (right), in Nebraska, 1934.

While Minnie was away, Hugh tried to sell the farmhouse plus thirteen acres. Minnie and Hugh had been planning to build a new home on the lower section of their property for some time. Hugh let people know the house was for sale and quickly found a buyer: Lizzie Erickson's twenty-six-year-old son, Elroy. After the sale Hugh moved into David's house near the tidelands.

From Elroy Erickson's perspective the old farmhouse was a shambles. Filled with years of accumulation, the house needed major cleaning and clearing. Before moving in, the Ericksons removed load after load of "stuff and junk" located both in and around the house.[6] While he was getting the place ready, Elroy had a survey done and discovered the property lines didn't match Hugh's description. Whether Hugh intentionally misled Elroy or made an honest mistake isn't clear. Louis Powers thought that the original property survey lines drawn on Depot Slough were off by a few yards, and that may have contributed to the confusion. Elroy put an immediate stop to the sale. Hugh returned their money, and the Ericksons moved out.[7] The families had been close neighbors for over fifteen years; after all the headaches were over they remained friends.

As Hugh worked through the sale and return of the farm, Alice Kyniston Murray faced a big decision. By 1934, Alice felt that she could no longer provide properly for her children. She decided to place them for adoption. The Murray family doesn't explain why David didn't ask for custody of his children. William (Bill) Joseph Murray was four years old; Barbara June, his little sister, was two.

77. The children of David and Alice Kyniston Murray: William Joseph Murray Wilken and Barbara June Murray Wilken in Grants Pass, Oregon, after their adoption, 1934.

The children soon found themselves with new parents, Emerson and Mildred Wilken from Grants Pass. The couple provided a loving, stable home where the children flourished.[8]

In 1935 Lucy was working at the Cooperage when she met and fell in love with co-worker Ben Wade. Ben worked as a stave sawyer. After a short courtship the couple married in 1935. Before long Lucy was pregnant. Family information about the couple is sketchy. Apparently Lucy and Ben struggled from the start. During the summer of 1936, Lucy lost her baby in childbirth while separated from Ben.[9] Subsequently, the couple divorced. Living alone in Toledo, Lucy invited Minnie to stay with her for a few months, appreciating her mother's support.

22
Notes

1. Louis Powers, interview by the author, taped, Toledo, Oregon, October 22, 2003.
2. Roy A. Green, interview by the author, written notes, Philomath, Oregon, July 9, 2003.
3. Alice Murray Green, "Memoirs."
4. Today this street is called Main Street.
5. The Bank Holiday took place in 1933 when President Franklin D. Roosevelt closed all banks in the United States March 6-10 to prevent depositors nationwide from withdrawing their money.
6. Betty Dickason, interview by the author, written notes, Siletz, Oregon, November 14, 2006.
7. Ibid.
8. Several decades passed before David Murray saw his children again.
9. Lucy's baby, named John Wade, died at birth. According to Roy Green, John was buried on the Murray farm in an unmarked grave.

23
"Lincoln County's First Hippie"

After three years of living in Toledo, Alice longed to leave town life behind and move back to the country:

> We had saved money to buy a place of our own. I was ready to take Dee and move out of town where there were open spaces, an old orchard, space for berries and all the produce to furnish good food, including a cow, poultry, calf and a pig. Roy was not a country boy but appreciated the acreage and the privacy.

Hugh and Minnie were growing older; he was sixty-eight, she was sixty-seven. Their ability to run the farm had diminished. Over the years Hugh had used many local boys to assist him with his projects: Pete, Kenneth, and Glen Roberts, Elroy and Lawrence Erickson, Marshall Clark, Louis Powers, and Rudy Thompson. But the day had arrived when both Hugh and Minnie wanted a quieter life with fewer demands.

In 1936, Hugh made Roy and Alice a proposition: if the couple would take care of him and Minnie in their old age, Hugh would deed over title to the old house plus thirteen acres of the farm. Roy and Alice agreed. During May that year Roy, Alice, and their two-year-old daughter, Dee, moved to the farm. Alice finally had the open space she'd been seeking:

> Dad and our family were living in the sadly neglected old house on the hill. Roy's interests were not in planting and growing. His interests were towards machinery. He wired the house for electricity, which our newly purchased light plant would furnish. Roy could run his shop machinery while we had good lights and a few appliances. Roy bought 900 feet of galvanized pipe. With eager Hugh's help, they piped pure cold spring water from high on the property. One bedroom was converted into a bathroom. It was papered, painted and new linoleum was laid before the fixtures were installed.
>
> The old house was re-floored, refinished inside and painted outside after new porches were finished, front and rear. Roy built a workshop adjoining the house for his machinery

and tools. Then he built a woodshed for wood and storage.

When Roy asked Hugh if he could have the old cider press, Hugh was happy to give it to him. Hugh appreciated watching Roy make all new wooden parts and repair the metal pieces. Roy enjoyed the fresh delicious cider.

78. The Green family: Twenty-eight-year-old Roy, thirty-year-old Alice, and four-year-old Dee, Toledo, Oregon, 1938.

Now settled, Alice faced a few challenges living back under the same roof with her father. Hugh's untidy habits eventually unraveled her patience. Unwilling to fight with her father, she vented her frustration to Roy, and in 1937 he spoke to Hugh:

We were quite comfortable living at the farm. There was one problem that affected peace in the family. Pretty near every day Hugh would come into the house with his boots covered in mud. Alice was trying to keep the house clean and was getting fed up because it was constantly getting filthy from all this mud. This went on for some time until Alice could not take it anymore. One day in the evening, I went over to Hugh and put my hand on his shoulder. I said, "Well, Hugh, I think this is it. You can't do much in there with the wife. She's pretty upset in there about it."

Hugh answered, "Well, I would like to know what *it* is?" and I answered, "I'll give you $1,000 to get out of here. I'll still take care of you until you are gone." He said that would be O.K. and that's what happened. We surveyed thirteen acres as our part of the farm, and he built a nice home just below our house.

The new arrangement suited everyone. Living *near* Hugh rather than *with* Hugh proved to be much easier for Alice. The families once again lived in peace.

79. Hugh Murray and his granddaughter, Dee, next to his and Minnie's new house, 1938.

About this time Lucy met a new man at the Cooperage. Jim Marrs, easy going and confident, made a good companion for the vivacious Lucy. The two began dating and Jim quickly became a favorite in Lucy's family.

While the Murrays were going through these transitions, Alice started her lifelong love of preserving family history. Although Hugh's personality stands out in the many family stories, Minnie's story is also compelling. To ensure Minnie's spirit wouldn't be forgotten, Alice asked her mother to fill out a personal profile card on Valentine's Day, 1937. Minnie was sixty-eight years old when she described herself:

My full name is Minnie Alice Owram Murray. I was born on October 2, 1868. My hair is dark brown, growing gray. My eyes are blue-gray. My height was 5 feet 6 ½ inches and I weighed 130 pounds. I am now only about 5 feet tall and weigh about 100 pounds.

I have had many favorite poems, favorite books & authors at different periods in my development. Also many hobbies at different times. (I didn't mention Numerology or Palmistry!).

Dogs are my favorite pets, but I like everything that may be liked. I like all the seasons, all kinds of weather, flowers, everything good to eat. I have no favorite cake or candy.

I like very much the poems of Robert Browning, E.B. Browning (his wife) and many more.

My hobbies are making gardens, both flower and vegetable, reading, writing and painting.

My ambitions are: to be of some use or do some good in the world. Also have wished to be a writer, especially of poetry.

The name of my church is nature, where I communicate directly with the infinite God. . . My favorite hymn: "Nearer My God to Thee."

Favorite Poem: Edwin Markham's "Man with the Hoe."

Favorite Book: Sir Edwin Arnold's *Light of Asia.*

Education I have had: Common School, age 8 to 15, and I have been learning ever since.

Minnie's brief biography supports the many stories about her contained in *Murray Loop.* She lost six and a half inches in height through age and the attack by the billy goat in 1925. Her love of books and good writing helped her reconnect with Hugh after moving from Liberal. She approached life as a constant opportunity to learn, appreciating nature and expressing her creativity. The literature she loved provides further insight into how Minnie thought of herself.

Her favorite poem, "The Man with the Hoe" (1899), was among the most popular of nineteenth-century American poems. Inspired by French artist Jean-Francois Millet's 1862 painting of the same name, the poem appeared in over 10,000 newspapers and magazines worldwide.[1] The farmer in the poem was thought to symbolize the working class burdened by work. The imagery of the poem spoke to Minnie, who had spent her life working the land.

On display at The Getty Center, Los Angeles, California

80. *Jean-Francois Millet:* The Man with the Hoe, *1862.*

Minnie remained an inherently positive woman. Her optimism is reflected in her favorite book, the 1880 bestseller *The Light of Asia.*[2] Written in verse by Sir Edwin Arnold, the book was America's introduction to Buddhism, a religion of universal hope, boundless love, and faith in good. *The Light of Asia* is a soothing counterpoint to "The Man with the Hoe."[3] Where Markham describes a dark and breaking world, Arnold tempers that world with hope. The contrasting ideas in these two works reveal the range of Minnie's thoughts and feelings.

Hugh was called a Renaissance man. For him, opening a book was like starting a conversation. He avidly participated in the writing:

> If you loaned Hugh Murray a book, when you got it back it was practically rewritten because he corrected the punctuation and spelling and explained by footnotes up and down the pages about this and that if he disagreed or had something to say about it. It was a very interesting thing.
>
> He had learned his spelling in Canada and that was the British version of spelling. And the pronunciation of a lot of these words.
>
> He was always concerned about certain words that he pronounced one way. To him, it wasn't correct the way us Yankees did it.[4]

Whether Hugh disagreed with the spelling, the grammar, or the ideas, he wrote his opinion as he read. Books were avenues to new ideas as well as discussions of old ones.

By 1937 the man who hadn't expected to grow old had turned seventy. His long hair reached down to his shoulders. He had, in fact, worn his hair shoulder length for much of his life after he turned thirty. He also had a beard that set him apart from the average clean-shaven man of his time. Louis Powers, who spent many weekends helping "Old Man Murray" with chores on the farm during the early 1930s, smiled when he referred to Hugh as "Lincoln County's first hippie."[5] Hugh's "look" went hand in hand with his character. But not everyone thought of him as a hippie.

In his later years Hugh split the linings of his vests and stuffed them with nuts, dried fruits, and apples to give to the children he met in his travels. The bottom of his vest bulged all around. In downtown Toledo one day, a child seeing Hugh's long hair, beard, and pockets full of fruit pointed excitedly and said, "Look Mama, Santa Claus."[6]

81. Hugh Murray and Wanda Grant, Honey Grove Road, Alsea, Oregon, ca. 1940.

Carol Ginter, a former Murray neighbor, recalled Hugh attending a Fourth of July celebration on her parents' farm during the early 1930s:

Hugh Murray, we called him "Old Man Murray". My main memory of Hugh

Murray was the way he looked, the way he played the fiddle, and he had a good personality. He was very approachable, especially with children. He always had stories to tell.

Our farms more or less joined. When we had the Fourth of July picnic on our farm, he brought his horse and buggy and would take all us kids for a ride. This probably would have been about 1933-34. We had cars then, so it was a big treat for us to get to ride in that buggy. Then he would play his fiddle.[7]

Children made an excited and appreciative audience. Hugh and Babe had been around long enough to become novelties to younger generations.

In July of 1937, Hugh took his fiddle on the road to Oregon's capital city, Salem. There he gained notoriety for Lincoln County when he won the statewide fiddle contest. The July 15 *Lincoln County Leader* colorfully detailed the event:

Hugh Murray Wins Fiddling Contest

With his waving silvery locks, cheerful smile and a good word for all, our good friend and neighbor, Hugh Murray, boxed his old time fiddle and motored to Salem where the American

Legion was sponsoring a 4th of July celebration, and as a special attraction, the night program was offering a $25.00 cash prize for the best old time fiddler. There was a lesser sum for second and third places. Twelve contestants had gathered for the occasion. . .

The chairman arose and to the huge audience said, "Friends, as the last number in this contest, I am pleased to introduce to you the venerable Hugh Murray of Toledo, Oregon.". . .

As his bow glided smoothly from string to string, and his fingers tattooed here and there in harmony with the bow, a glance over the audience convinced him that it was with him. Never before in his 56 years of fiddling had he appeared before a more apparently appreciative audience. . .

He was pronounced winner and received the $25.00 cash award.

With thanks, he received his prize and as a parting remark said, "Just tell them that that Siwash brave from the Sitka Spruce Country of Siletz Bay region went on the warpath and scalped the other braves at the old fiddlers contest."

After wrangling the largest amount of wampum, he proceeded home with his booty. He says the American boys are "Skookum Bucks."

Fully confident with a fiddle in hand, Hugh knew he was good, and he savored playing to the crowd.

The next summer, the old apple orchard had a bounty of apples ready for harvest. Many were already on the ground when Louis Powers visited one day and talked with Hugh:

> He'd been up to our place and knew we had pigs. He asked, "You want some apples?" And I says, "What would I do with them?" And he says, "Feed them to your pigs." He said that they were just going to rot. So we took the apples up there. He had a couple of barrels. They were old steel drums, oil barrels with the ends cut off. I was going to take them back to him but he said to keep them for feed barrels. So I got the next-door neighbor to haul them up there for me. Mom picked out a lot of good apples. She made apple cider out of them. She made several gallons. The ones that were no good, they went to the pigs. Before we got to the bottom of the barrel the apples began to ferment. The pigs got high and they were chasing each other around and rooting each other. They rolled over. Oh man, they went nuts.

The neglected apples resulted from changing times. With no one to pick crops and follow a market route, the orchard's harvest went to waste. Since the Murrays, young and old, no longer centered their lives around the farm, Mrs. Powers made the cider Alice and Lucy once worked to produce, and someone else's pigs grew fat on the rich, sweet leftovers.

82. *Hugh Murray and Babe, 1938. Hugh wrote on the back of the photograph: "This picture was taken by a neighbor lady as I worked there. Babe is in her 24th year and too active for the benefit of my old rheumatic frame."*

As Hugh prepared for quieter days he no longer needed Babe, the family workhorse for over twenty years. With no more crops to plant, Hugh offered to give Babe to Louis Powers:

I was about 18 when Hugh gave me his horse, Babe. He didn't have anymore use for it. We had to get wood off the hill on our property, and he said, "Take my horse up there. If I need it I'll come up and get it." We had forty acres for the horse to run in if it needed to. So we took the horse up there and pulled wood off of the hill. Hugh come up and he was visiting with us and he says, "Well, how is your horse doing?" And I said "My horse?" He says, "He's yours if you want him. I have no use for him anymore." So he gave me the horse.

Babe was real gentle. Shoot, the kids could crawl underneath that horse and grab a hold of the horse's back legs or front legs and it would never kick. I never knew it to kick. Once in a while it would get a rock in its foot. I'd pick her foot up and take the rock out, and she never offered to kick. I have seen horses where you pick up their back feet, they would kick ya, or if you pick their front foot up, they would paw at ya. But Babe, she never did.

When Cliff Helmer's horse passed away, Cliff only had one and his horse wouldn't work single. Hugh's horse worked single or double, pulling wagons or anything. It was harder to plow one horse instead of two. So, when Cliff's horse passed away, I took Babe out there. Cliff was really happy, and those two horses got along good together and worked together. He had Babe about five years and then she finally died.

Babe, like the old orchard, had served the Murrays well.

Hugh broke his arm twice during his years on the farm. The first time a neighbor set the break in a homemade splint. Lucy writes that during its healing the family had little success in keeping Hugh from continuing his antics:

> Dad talked and gestured and bounced around, moving the broken arm up and down in its tea towel sling. Of course, we all kept hollering at him, "Dad, your broken arm, hold it still!"

The second time Hugh broke his arm was years later. His son-in-law Roy Green set the break, and it healed perfectly.

With little interest in the farm, Hugh spent more time indulging in his hobbies: playing the fiddle, sharing his latest literary finds with Minnie, and talking with friends. Of the three, talking topped Hugh's list. Jackie Robeson recalled: "Hugh Murray liked to talk. If you walked in downtown Toledo, quite often you would see him on a street corner talking to someone."[8]

Years earlier Minnie, Alice, and Lucy had overheard two workmen chatting about Hugh near their property. One of the men asked, "Who lives in that house?" The other man replied, "That's the wife and daughters of that fellow they call the human talking machine."[9] Lucy doubted anyone ever called Hugh a "talking machine" to his face but agreed the label fit. Alice had long felt she understood the cause of Hugh's constant chatter: "Father was inclined to talk loudly and at length. He possessed an overly strong vein of pride." But Hugh's pride soon received a terrible blow.

As Hugh, who had spent a lifetime fighting chronic illness, moved ably around visiting friends and playing the fiddle, his spirited companion of thirty-three years fell ill. The robust woman who had walked with such a decisive clip in her younger days had withered to frailty and illness. Minnie soon took to her bed. By December 1938 she was too weak to care for herself.

83. Hugh Murray talking to Mr. Gentry on Main Street, Toledo, Oregon, 1939.

23
Notes

1. David R. Weimer, "On Edwin Markham's 'The Man with the Hoe,'" in *Literature, Class, and Culture: An Anthology*, eds. Paul Lauter and Ann Fitzgerald (New York: Longman, 2001). http://www.english.illinois.edu/maps/poets

2. Edwin Arnold, *The Light of Asia: The Life and Teaching of Gautama* (Boston: Roberts Brothers, 1880).

3. Edwin Markham, *The Man with the Hoe and Other Poems* (New York: Doubleday & McClure Co., 1899).

4. Rudy Thompson, telephone interview by the author, August 13, 2007.

5. Louis Powers, interview by the author, Newport, Oregon, August 22, 2006.

6. Lucy Murray Marrs, "Memoirs."

7. Carol Ginter to the author, 11 January 2006.

8. Jackie Robeson, interview by the author, Toledo, Oregon, December 5, 2003.

9. Marrs, "Memoirs."

24
The Death of Minnie Murray

Roy and Alice had long planned a two-week family vacation to visit the 1939 San Francisco World's Fair and Exposition. Minnie's continued illness made them question their plans. With heartfelt reservations they decided to go. Roy later explained that before leaving, he and Alice arranged for long-time friend Etta Burch Helmer to care for Minnie:

> In July 1939, Alice and I took a two-week vacation. Before we left on our trip, I hired a family friend to stay at our house and take care of Minnie. She was seventy-one years old and quite ill. We had brought her up from the house below. An extra bed was placed in her room for the caretaker.

Alice was torn between the excitement of the expo and concern for her mother. Without a phone at the farm, Alice couldn't call to check on how Minnie was doing. Roy remembered Alice's anxiety:

When we returned home, Alice first went to see Minnie. She was so weak, all she could do was look up and say, "Oh, it's you Alice." Alice said, "Yeah, Mom, it's me," and gave her a big hug.

Alice and Roy had returned in time to say good-bye. The following day Minnie passed away. The woman who had faced life with courage, kindness, and hope was gone.

The family went about quietly preparing her body for burial:

We cleaned her and dressed her up real nice. Before she died, Hugh had given Dave $5 to buy wood for her coffin which he made real nice. Alice and Lucy lined it with pillows and a bedspread. Then the coffin was placed on the back porch. Her remains lay there for two days.[1]

The back entrance was the main way in and out of the house. Here the family could view and mourn her as they prepared for her burial. They planned to bury Minnie on the farm, as she had wanted.

During this early stage of grief the Murrays sheltered themselves in privacy, deciding to keep Minnie's passing quiet as they dealt with her loss. Their decision had unfortunate consequences.

Minnie's longtime friend Lizzie Erickson had not been told of Minnie's passing. Charles Burch described Lizzie's shock when she discovered her friend's body:

> This old lady Erickson lived over the hill towards where my folks lived, and she used to visit back and forth. She decided to go down and visit the Murrays. She come down over the hill, walked up there on the porch, and here was this nice box sitting there. She walked over and opened it up. They said that she hollered all the way home going over the hill. It damn near scared her to death. I was eighteen years old but remember that like it was yesterday.

In recalling this incident, Rudy Thompson said that Hugh had planned to bury Minnie on the farm. Upon discovering this plan Lizzie reacted strongly, saying, "Hugh, you can't do that." Hugh ignored her. So when Lizzie got home she contacted the county coroner. The next morning the coroner came to the house and demanded that Minnie be embalmed or buried within twenty-four hours. With an abrupt change in plans, Roy and David drove to Newport and made arrangements for Minnie to be buried in Eureka Cemetery.[2]

When planning her funeral, Minnie had requested a simple service with singing. David asked Adelaide Adams, a woman he was dating at the time, and Verne Ross, one of Minnie's long-time friends from Toledo, to sing at the memorial. Alice writes that she and Lucy did the rest of the arranging:

> David asked a splendid singer, Adelaide Adams, Siletz Indian,[3] and well known little lady Verne Ross to lead the singing of a few of Minnie's favorite songs. She had expressed a wish for two or three songs. I fashioned wreaths and sprays of her roses and cedar branches. Friends brought some florists pots and flowers. I did not realize my loss for weeks, and then it was too late to weep.

Years later, Hugh recalls in his diary his memories of Minnie's funeral:

> . . . my Sweetheart "Minnie". She left the worn and crippled little body in July 1939, and one of the hymns that she chose to be sung at her graveside [included the following line]: "There's a land that is fairer than day, and by faith we can see it afar. Where our

father waits over the waves to prepare us a dwelling place there."

The woman who through nature communicated "directly with the infinite God" was sent to her rest with music proclaiming the peace of a faithful heart.

On August 3, 1939, The *Lincoln County Leader* printed Minnie's obituary:

Mrs. H. Murray Buried in Newport Cemetery July 21

Mrs. Hugh Murray, resident of this section for the past forty years, passed away July 20th after an eight-month illness.

Minnie Owram was born at Berlin Heights, Ohio in October 1868. She came to Oregon with her mother and was married to Hugh Murray in 1905. He came from Missouri here.

To this union were born David Murray, Mrs. Alice Green and Lucy Wade, all residing at Toledo. She is survived by her husband and three grandchildren beside the three children.

Mrs. Murray cared little for pomp and display and by her special request only a song service was held at the graveside in the Newport cemetery on July 21, where about sixty of her relatives and friends gathered to pay tribute and cover her grave with flowers.

The obituary fails to capture the essence of Minnie's life. Missing is any mention of her independence, creativity, energy, self-confidence, and loyalty to family. Nor does the summary mention the hole left in a family grieving for her.

Minnie had lived a demanding but fulfilling life. She stood out as an unusual woman. Unwilling to blindly conform to custom or tradition, she cut her hair and shortened her skirts at a time when society advocated long hair and longer hems. In the 1880s, while still in her teens, she ran a photography business in Missouri. In the 1890s she sold her quick-portrait sketches, pastels, and fine handicraft artwork to the bustling summer tourist trade in Newport, Oregon. The 1900 U.S. Census lists Minnie's profession as "Crayon Artist." She enjoyed being on the water and rowed alone up and down the Yaquina River to camp and paint nature scenes. She bought a home in Toledo and throughout her adult life supported her mother. After her marriage, she became a faithful companion to her husband and a loving, playful mother to her children.

Neighbor Rudy Thompson recalled Minnie as an active farm wife during the early 1920s:

> Minnie was a pretty good artist, I know that. She used to paint Easter cards and Christmas cards and peddle them in the neighborhood. She did some scenes, like along the water, bulrushes, the water, cattails, little scenic things on the Easter cards. She really was a pretty good artist.
>
> She was a terrific gardener too. She had a little wagon that she got from my folks. She used to load that thing up, pull it down to Toledo, and peddle those fresh vegetables around Toledo.

Many people had fond memories of this kind and spirited woman. After Minnie's passing, Lucy visited Postmaster Rosemary Schenck at the Toledo Post Office one day. Rosemary, who had attended the Murrays' wedding, had been friends with Minnie for almost forty years. With her usual candor, she told Lucy that neither she nor her sister Alice could "hold a candle" to their mother. Rosemary said that "Minnie in her younger years moved so fast, people just heard the snap of her skirt as she went out of sight around a corner." [4]

84. Minnie and Hugh Murray, 1936.

Louis Powers recalled Hugh and Minnie's relationship in the early 1930s:

> I never saw Minnie come out of the house when I was visiting or helping Hugh on the farm. Minnie stayed inside the house cooking and keeping

herself busy. If she needed something from Hugh, she would go to the back porch, which the family used as the entrance to the house, and either call out or ring a bell to get Hugh's attention.

Minnie was good at speaking her mind and letting Hugh know how she felt and Hugh respected Minnie. I never saw Minnie grouchy. She was always friendly toward me. I don't think she had an enemy.

I enjoyed spending time at the Murray farm and often volunteered my work in exchange for meals.[5]

Minnie had held her own against her strong-willed, outspoken husband. She had faced Hugh with subtlety and determination. He in turn had listened to what she had to say. They had made their marriage work, and Hugh, more than anyone, felt Minnie's absence. He missed sharing his various readings and discussing his thoughts with her. After thirty-four years with Minnie, Hugh felt empty without his beloved companion. The loss never left him.

To combat his loneliness, Hugh spent more time visiting Alice. He also made changes in his home. With so much empty and unused space in his house, Hugh decided to live in one room while renting out the rest. This paid the property taxes and gave him a modest income.

As Hugh and the family dealt with the death of Minnie and the changes brought by her passing, Lucy solidified her connection to the love of her life. She married James B. Marrs in October 1939.

Minnie Owram Murray through Seven Decades

1871

1884

1891

1906

1913

ca.1925

1936

24
Notes

1. Roy A. Green, interview by the author, Philomath, Oregon, July 9, 2003.
2. Gene Bateman, interview by the author, Newport, Oregon, October 25, 2007. Today Lincoln County property owners must get permission from adjoining landowners for a private burial site, then dedicate a portion of their land to make a cemetery. In 1939 the requirement was not on the books. People such as Lizzie Erickson who objected to private property burial could only try to discourage their neighbors from doing so.
3. Robert Kentta, Cultural Resource Director of the Confederated Tribes of Siletz, has a number of interesting stories about Adelaide Adams, who was his great aunt.
4. Lucy Murray Marrs, "Sketch of Mrs. Hugh Murray," 1978.
5. Louis Powers, interview by the author, Corvallis, Oregon, March 14, 2007.

25
Old Man Murray—"Vaccinated by a phonograph needle."

As the 1940s opened, family surrounded Hugh. His sister Emma retired after a long teaching career and moved into a house next to the Murray property. In August 1941 baby Nancy was born to Alice and Roy. Alice described Nancy as a "large blonde baby doll." Dee was seven years old. Lucy and her husband Jim Marrs soon moved to Corvallis, fifty miles to the east.

At the start of World War II, Hugh paid a visit to David, who was working near Fresno, California, and taking care of a vineyard.

*85. Hugh Murray playing the fiddle at his son
David's home near Fresno, California, ca.
1940.*

To give Hugh something to do during his visit, David helped him get a job at a war plant:

> His job was to sort out nuts and bolts and put each size in a separate box. When he had done this, he discovered that the Foreman took them away, dumped them all back together again, and brought them back to him to re-sort. Immediately, Hugh became furious. His Scottish blood began to

boil, and he had very bad words with the Foreman, saying he was going to let the head of their Division know what the Foreman had done. The latter told Hugh he was only following orders, and that Hugh would be laughed out of the plant, or fired outright for fomenting trouble. So Hugh stormed out of there in a rage, never to return.[1]

Hugh wanted no part of killing time. Dissatisfied, he returned to Oregon.

86. Hugh Murray reading in his house on Murray Loop, ca. 1947.

Back home, Hugh spent his time visiting friends. Wherever he went, he carried his violin. He rarely finished playing a tune before stopping to tell a story. Rudy Thompson compared Hugh's story-telling to floating down a river. Starting at the river's source, Hugh stopped along the way to describe each tributary in detail. Hugh always got sidetracked before completing his main subject.[2] Rudy wasn't the only one to notice Hugh's rambling. Louis Powers had his own way of describing Hugh's constant conversation:

> Old Hugh Murray, a lot of people said that he got vaccinated by a phonograph needle. He never shut up. Even in his sleep I think that he would talk. Him and I were buddies.[3]

In 1944, Hugh's sister-in-law, Hattie Starr, died at eighty-two. Hattie had been a widow for twenty-one years and an active participant in the Toledo community since the 1890s when she and Lester had moved to Oregon from Kansas. Ralph, Ina and Hamilton Sturdevant's son, died in 1945. He had lived away from his family for many years, so he had few ties to the local community.

Two years later Emma Murray died. She had never married but spent her life around children as a schoolteacher. She lived her last few years close by her older brother Hugh and next door to her nephew David.

In 1949, Hugh's old friend Bill Bredstead wrote a letter asking Hugh for help. Bill was a family friend from years earlier when he had lived in Toledo. About 1940 he bought a ranch near Wallowa in the far northeast section of Oregon. In 1949 his wife left him. Bill wrote Hugh to ask if he would spend some time at his ranch. Hugh agreed and traveled east by bus.

A few days after arriving, Hugh wrote the following letter to Lucy:

> Lucy Marrs
> 1971 Taylor St.
> Corvallis, Oregon
> Saturday June 11th 1949
>
> My Dear Girlie Lucy. Here I am: since a few days.
> Bill Bredstead wrote that his more or less "wife" flew the coop.
> Worst was [she] took his 11 year old daughter out of school and decamped with his car. He asked if I might be able to come up here some time in summer. So, I wrote [that I] would come soon as

possible and asked for directions to find him.

His daughter is a large strong girl for her age. She is an accomplished horse girl. He let her ride and drive his team. So she became a great help in haying and furrowing.

His "wife" sued for divorce, asking $75 month alimony. Practically everything that he owned. . .

He rents a big wild ranch, milking of cows and feeding and watering 50 pigs and their dams. Sells some eggs but must carry eggs and cream ¾ of a mile to truck line. He is not well and is sadly overworked besides the heartbreak . . .

He has to lug the milk uphill to separator. Lug the skimmed milk down to hogs and lug all water uphill from a leaky pump that is so worn it must be primed with a half gallon of water for every pail he pumps while carrying it to the hog trough.

The tendon that I tore on right shoulder still pains and cripples me and my worn hands and arms, so that I barely can milk what I can drink. . .

Except on the prairies east of Rocky Mountains, this place provides the wildest view of anywhere I lived in the 80 years of my remembrance. . .

I enclose a wild rose (pink) and some blue wild flowers. Have no pink ones on hand. . .

Ever, your old pest and burden.
"Payshins" [4]

Address me here as:
H. Murray, Wallowa, Oregon
c/o Wm Bredstead

Hugh stayed on Bill's ranch for five weeks. On July 6, 1949, the two of them spent a busy day tending animals. In the evening when they were returning to the house, Bill noticed some cattle had gotten loose. He tended to the wayward stock while an exhausted Hugh went inside. After removing his shoes, Hugh sat down in the front room with pencil and paper in hand. He wrote the following letter:

July 6th 1949
Wallowa, Oregon

My Dear Alice and all of you,

We had thunder and lightning last evening, and perhaps ¼ inch of rain. But not much use as everything is too dry and is too late in season to help the wheat and hay. . .

[Not having a] car is hell for Bill. He used it to pull up the horse forks of hay from wagon. . . He offers half his hay crop to a neighbor to stack his half. Neighbor looked at it, then declined. . . don't see what he can do, me so helpless!. . .

The pain in my stomach comes on with less and less cause. . . It first started from exertion when I was grubbing out the spruce. . . Even a walk after cows brings a dull ache that sweats me. . .

Please pay our dear Nancy if she will water the grape cuttings, plum-sprouts and redwood cuttings. . . One grape cutting is near the road by the broom handle fence. . . The other is in shade of a little apple tree . . .

Hope you pay Nancy . . . But tell Nancy to . . . hoe my strawberry plants if she is able.

Best Wishes and do not over work,
Pa Hugh

The sky had darkened by the time Bill returned to the house. He saw Hugh sitting in the front room with the letter in his hand and called out to him. When Bill received no response he knew Hugh was gone. Bill arranged to send the body home. Two days later he wrote his own letter to Alice:

July 8th, 1949
Wallowa

Dear Friends,

I am hereby sending you my sympathy.
I know you have lost a good Dad and
Grandad. . . and I feel the loss of a very
good friend.

[Hugh] liked to pick the wild flowers
and look at the snow capped
mountains and he was good at doing
little chores that needed to be taken
care of, such as feeding and watering
the little chicks. He would bring in milk
cows.

The evening of the 6th, after feeding
the pigs and separating the milk, we
went to the house to get some supper. I
looked to the north end of [the] place. I
could see that some of the beef cattle
had broke into a wheat field. So I told
him I would go and put them back in
the pasture. He said he guessed he
wouldn't be able to help me much if he
went with me, so he went to the house.

When I got back it was getting dark.
After entering the house, I called him,
but no answer. I walked into [the] front
room. I could see him sitting in a
rocking chair. He had taken his shoes
off. I went over and put my hand on his
shoulder and spoke to him, no answer.

369

I took his hand in mine. I knew then that he was dead.

I ran to a neighbor about 1-½ miles away, but there was no one home, so I went on another half mile to Mr. Temples. He took me to Wallowa. We went to the Doctor. He phoned to Mr. Booth in Enterprise.

I will send violin, money and things that are left here as soon as I can.

Your friend,
Bill

When Hugh's coffin arrived in Toledo, Roy, his son-in-law, took the remains to the Parker Funeral Home in Newport. Hugh was laid to rest beside Minnie in Eureka Cemetery. The family held a private service with only immediate relatives present for the burial. Lucy describes in third person what her father would have thought of Parker's preparation:

When his children got together at the Parker Funeral Home in Newport, Oregon, there his body lay in a casket, all decked out in a neat, modern brown suit, donated by Mr. Parker. His hair all neatly combed, no flowers in it, no hat with flowers or a feather in the hatband, and shoes on his feet . . . Oh, would he ever have blustered about that waste of good clothing, poking it down in a hole in the ground to rot, when someone in need could have been getting good use of it!

Lucy understood her father's philanthropic and frugal nature. Talented, talkative, generous, friendly, and grumpy, Hugh was another complex Murray. Although his relationships with his wife and children were sometimes turbulent, he had loved each of them.

In their own way Minnie and Hugh made a good match. They loved each other perhaps because they were so different, yet they shared common values. Neither married until their late 30s. They each had talents and interests that had nothing to do with farming. Both were philosophical, interested in the betterment of society and community. Both were creative, independent spirits who enjoyed spontaneity. They were also contrasting personalities. Hugh was quick tempered and sometimes intolerant while Minnie was gentle and forbearing. Hugh tried to establish family roles based on gender, but he couldn't dominate his even-tempered wife. Together they reared a family as capable and original as themselves, while also passing down the characteristics and ideals so much a part of both family lines.

The Murrays were a unique collection of individuals. As Rudy Thompson put it, "Everybody in the family was interesting in one way or another."

25
Notes

1. Lucy Murray Marrs, "Sketch of Mr. Hugh Murray," 1978.
2. Rudy Thompson to the author, 25 August 2007.
3. Louis Powers, interview by the author, Toledo, Oregon, October 22, 2003.
4. Popeye the Sailor, an impatient fictional hero with a speech impediment, first appeared in a 1929 comic strip and later became a popular cartoon character who would sometimes say, "I gots plenty of payshins at all times." Since Hugh's reputation didn't include being long on patience, "Payshins" became one of his pet names.

APPENDIX

Ted W. Cox

88. The graves of Minnie and Hugh Murray overlook the Pacific Ocean. From 1949 to 2005 Roy Green took flowers to their graves every Memorial Day (except when he and Alice were out of the state from 1952 to 1968). Since Roy's passing in 2005, the author has gone in his place, trimming the flowers with Roy's pocketknife.

89. *Lucy Murray Marrs and Alice Murray Green with freshly pulled turnips from a friend's garden on the Toledo—Siletz Road near their old family farm, 1986. When Alice and Lucy were in their teens, they pulled stock beets and turnips from their tideland garden each afternoon and carried them in sacks up to the barn where the vegetables were chopped up and fed to the cows.*

Ted W. Cox

90. In this 2007 photograph, Patricia Sturdevant Dye holds the pastel printed on the cover of Murray Loop. *The picture was drawn circa 1897 by Minnie Owram, her great-great-aunt. It hung in Ina Sturdevant's house for over thirty years, and after she died in 1928, her grandson Frank got possession of the work. Frank owed a friend some money and gave the man the drawing to settle the debt. For fifty years the delicate pastel was protected from sunlight while it was stored in an attic. In 1991, after sixty-three years, the pastel was given to Patricia, thus returning it to the family. Today, the beautiful work is displayed at the Lincoln County Museum, Newport, Oregon.*

91. Two-year old Ted W. Cox at 10 N. Ash. Street, Eugene, Oregon, with a bear cub rescued from a logging operation in the Coburg Hills near Eugene, summer 1949.

INDEX

A

B

Blue, Lucy F., 85
Bogart, Eleanor, 319
Boone Slough, 145,146
Booth, Mr., 370
Brainard, Mr., 60
Bredstead, Billl, 365,369
Brookes, Louise, 276
Burch,
    Charles, xxix,260,270,273,303,304,351
    Chester, 196
    Effie, 283,285,295,296
Burgess, Dr. R.D., 159,160,164,320
Burlington Flats, New York, 57
Butter tubs, 299,304

C

Canady, Lois, 253
Case, Samuel, 77,79,163
Champoeg, 17,18,27
Chautauqua, New York, 50,163
Chiloquin, Oregon, 266
Christian Science, 131,132
Clark, Marshall, 327
Clay County, Kansas, 62,103,132,163
Clearances, 4
Cliff House, 192
Collins, George, 74
Collins, Mr., 186
Conductor, Underground Railroad, 61
Confederated Tribes of Siletz, xxiii

Copeland, J.S., 83
Cosgrove, Ted, 315
Coquelle, John, 75
Cromarty, Scotland, 2,5
Crabtree, Oregon, 283,285,296
Crawford,
   Hugh (1782-Unk), 45
   Mary Ann (1815-Unk), 49
   Nancy Phedora (1824-1907),
   Vina (1819-Unk), 46,49,93,94,95,97,
     98,105
   Wilder (1827-Unk), 45
Creamery Package Manufacturing Co.,
   299,301,302

D
Dahl Dam, 249
Damon, Mr., 190
Dart, Anson (1797-1879), 20,21,22,23
Darwin, xvi,54,114
Davis, Mr., 267
Dixon, James, 89
Drift Creek, 148,158
Duke of Sutherland, 2,10

E
Elk City, Oregon, 78,85,126
England,
   Barnsley, xvii,56,93
   Liverpool, 93

Graves, Willard, 248,255,246
Gray,
   Russell, 287,291,292
   Will, 287,295
Great Britain, 13,17,25,27
Green,
   Alice Phedora (1907-1998),
   Bill (1912-1998), 315
   Dolores L. (1934-1989), 327,361,320
   Nancy (b.1941), 222,282,361,368
   Roy (1910-2005),

H

Hammer, Butch, 80
Harmony Hall, 113
Hedges, Absalom (1817-1890), 34
Helmer,
   Cliff, 343
   Etta (Burch), 349
Henningson, Peter, 218
Hogg, Egenton T., 126
Homestead,7,8,15,16,19,20,62, 66,67,82,
     86,132,148,158
Hudson Bay Company, 17

I

Indians,
   Alsea, 31,74
   Athabaskan, 24
   Chetco, 33,90

J
Johnson, Andrew, 72
Juliet, 70

K
Kansas,
  Clay County, 62,103,132,163
Keiffer, Mr., 206
Kellogg, George, 78,85,92
Kentta, Robert, xxiii,90,360
Kilburn,
  Mary, 102
  Celia, 101,103
Kyniston,
  Alice, (1911-1986), 284,323,324
  Herb, 238
  Lee, 238
  William, 284

L
Lady Gray, 5,6,7
Lane, Joseph (1801-1881), 18-20
Lea, Luke (1783-1851), 22
Leveson-Gower, Grainville, 2
Lightbody, James A., 111,284
Lincoln County, 130
Liverpool, England, 93
Lords of Themselves, xxi
Ludlow & Company, 71

M

Isabella (1831- Unk), 5,8
Lucy Margaret (1910-2007),
Lydia Sellers (1835-1919), 8,110,120,
    166,231,232
Margaret (1836-1918), 5
Minnie Owram (1868-1939),
Sarah (1866-1924), 8
Simon (1872-1955), 111,121,166,168,
    170,172,173

N

Nairn, 10
National Bank Holiday, 318
Nelson, Anthony, 153,166,232,321
Nesmith, James, 72
Newsome, David, 80
Newspapers,
    Appeal to Reason, 116,220
    Benton Democrat, 89
    Corvallis Gazette, 75,78,83
    Lincoln County Leader, 155,163,170,
        284,317,339,353
    Oregon Statesman, 29
    Spokesman Review, 220
    The Family Herald, 220
    Weekly Star, 220
    *Yaquina Bay News,*135
Newport, Oregon, xxiii,38,75-77,80,81,86,
        88,126,128,133,140,144,147,190-
        192,207,234,278,351,353,354,370

North Beach, Oregon, 76,79,81
Nortons, Oregon, 72,78,81
Nova Scotia, Canada, xvii,6,63,107,108
Nye Beach, Oregon, 140,190,192,290

O

Ocean House, 76-79,88
Odeneal, 72
Old Woman Creek, Ohio, 59
Olalla Valley, Oregon, 207,211,246
Oregon,
    Country, 13,14,16,17,18,25,27
    Donation Land Act, 20,66
    Territory, 21
Oysters, 70,71,234
Oysterville, 86,87,171
Owram,
    Joseph (1826-1886), xvii,56,64,66,93,
      88,93
    Minnie Alice (1868-1939)
    Nancy (Jennie) P. (1824-1907)

P

Pacific Northwest, 129
Pacific Spruce Sawmill, 272
Palmer, Joel (1810-1888), 23,29,30-34,38
Parker Funeral Home, 370
Peterson, A.T., 198
Pierce, Franklin, 31
Pioneer (steam boat), 78,79,83,85

Pioneer City, Oregon, 79,87,91,92,75,78
Powers, Louis, 313,322,327,337,341,342,
	356,364
Premier Sawmill, 83,84
Provisional Government, 18,27,28
Public Domain, 19,24,29

R
Railroads,
	Corvallis & Eastern, 147
	Oregon Pacific, 125,135
	Southern Pacific, 127,135,202,211,262
	Siletz Railroad and Navigation, 198,252
	Transcontinental, 125
	Willamette Valley and Coast, 125
Rational Dress Society, xviii,116
Rialto, 83,84
Richards, Audrey, 275,276
Roberts,
	Glen, 290,327
	Kenneth, 327
	Pete, 327
Robeson, Jackie, 344
Romtvedt, Borgny (1892-1985), 208,213
Ross, Verne, 303,352
Ross-shire, 10

S
Salisbury,
	Burt, 285

Vera Len(1883-1975), 103,129
Jennie (Nancy) (1824-1907)
Stanton Country School, 207,208,211,215,
224,226,235,237,243,246
Sturdevant,
Hamilton, (1836-1908), 62,130,132,
138,264,284,364
Ina, (1849-1928), 47,50,52,62,103,
130,132,133,134,137,138,162,
264,284,364,376
*Sunset Magazine,*171,201,202,210,211
Sunrise School, 107
Superintendent of Indian Affairs
Joseph Lane, 18,19,20
Anson Dart, 20,21,22,23
Joel Palmer, 23,29,30,31,33,34,38
Sutherland, Duke, 2,10
Sweetbriar School, 252,264
Sylvia Beach Hotel, 192,193

T
Thatcher's Barbershop, 317
Thomas, Joe, 266
Thompson, Rudy (b. 1912), 177,185,210,
237, 253,255,263,278,327,351,355,
364,372
Thorn, Mrs., 79
Thurston, Samuel (1815-1851), 19
Tillinghast, O.C., 60
Toledo Lumber Company, 199

Toney River District, Nova Scotia, 7
Turner, Oregon, 287,292

W
Wade,
    Ben, 325
    John (1936-1936), 326
Wagon road, Corvallis/Yaquina, 72,73,78,
        85,92
Walser, George H., 113,115,132
War, Rogue River, 33
White, Elijah (1806-1879), 16,19,27
Wilder, Mary, 45
Wilken,
    Bill (b.1929), 324
    Emerson, 324
    Barbara (b.1932), 324
    Mildred, 324
Willapa Bay, 70
Winant & Company, 71,87
Winchell,
    Edwin, 63
    Susan, 103